*Seventh Edition*

# Mass Communication Law in Arkansas

Bruce L. Plopper, Ph.D.
Stephen D. Ralph, J.D.

Copyright © 2012 by New Forums Press, Inc.

All rights reserved. No part of this publication may be reproduced or transmitted in any form or by any means, electronic or mechanical, including photocopy, or any information storage or retrieval system, without written permission from the publisher.
This book may be ordered in bulk quantities at discount from New Forums Press, Inc., P.O. Box 876, Stillwater, OK 74076
[Federal I.D. No. 73-11232391]

ISBN 10: 1-58107-218-X
ISBN 13: 978-1-581072-18-1

# Table of Contents

# About the Authors

BRUCE L. PLOPPER teaches undergraduate and graduate classes in the School of Mass Communication at the University of Arkansas at Little Rock. He specializes in mass communication law and journalism history, but he also teaches a variety of other courses.

Dr. Plopper earned his B.S. degree in psychology from Michigan State University, his M.A. degree in psychology from Southern Illinois University in Carbondale, and his Ph.D. degree in journalism from Southern Illinois University in Carbondale.

STEPHEN D. RALPH is an attorney living in Conway, Ark., and practicing criminal law. He has taught college courses in media and in radio-TV production, and he currently teaches media law and ethics at the University of Central Arkansas.

Mr. Ralph has a B.S. degree in radio and television and an M.A. degree in speech communication from the University of Illinois. He received a J.D. degree from the Bowen School of Law at the University of Arkansas at Little Rock.

# Arkansas Media Organizations

In any state, individual media outlets are strengthened by organizations that provide their members with information and educational opportunities to grow, develop, and effectively compete in the marketplace. The Arkansas news media are served by a variety of organizations, such as the Arkansas Broadcasters Association, Arkansas Press Women, Arkansas Scholastic Press Association, and the Society of Professional Journalists.

The oldest trade association in the state, however, is the Arkansas Press Association, which was formed in 1873 and is located in Little Rock. In addition to its more than 140 newspaper members, there are about 100 associate members, including advertising agencies, educators, and others interested in affiliating with the newspaper industry.

As part of its mission to keep its members informed, the APA each year conducts two conventions, as well as a dozen seminars and conferences. It also publishes a weekly newsletter, a quarterly magazine, and an annual media directory. Its staff and members lead the Freedom of Information Coalition in Arkansas, a group that can be found at the forefront of efforts to preserve open meetings and open records.

# Preface

This text is designed to provide diverse audiences with information about the history and current legal status of typical mass communication issues in Arkansas. It is useful as a supplemental text for mass communication law classes taught at the state's various colleges and universities, and it also serves as a practical guide for high school journalism teachers and advisers, mass media professionals, and attorneys who specialize in areas outside of mass communication law.

The Arkansas Constitution, state statutes, and Arkansas Supreme Court decisions form the primary basis for discussion of mass communication law in Arkansas. On occasion, federal court decisions and other decisions from lower courts in Arkansas provide additional background.

Although this text does not contain a chapter devoted specifically to broadcast law and regulation, legal issues involving broadcasting in Arkansas are included in nearly every chapter.

Citations in the text and in the references sections refer to several legal sources. The most frequently cited source of state statutes is the *Arkansas Code Annotated,* cited as A.C.A. and followed by a set of three numbers and a date, e.g., A.C.A. 25-19-101 *et seq.* (1987). This refers to Title 25, Chapter 19, Section 101 and those sections that follow, of the *Arkansas Code Annotated* of 1987 (the last time the full Arkansas Code was revised). References to the code include all changes in the laws made by the Arkansas General Assembly since 1987. Citations to federal law are made to U.S.C.A., which refers to United States Code Annotated.

When court decisions are involved, the most frequently cited sources are the *Arkansas Reports* (Ark. and Ark. 2d) and the *Southwestern Reporter* (S.W., S.W.2d, and S.W.3d), for Arkansas Supreme Court decisions; the *Federal Supplement* (F. Supp. and F. Supp. 2d), for federal district court decisions; the *Federal Reporter* (F., F.2d, and F.3d), for decisions from various circuits of the U.S. Court of Appeals; and *United States Reports* (U.S.) and the *Supreme Court Reporter* (S.Ct.), for United States Supreme Court decisions.

The Arkansas Supreme Court on May 28, 2009, announced that after Feb. 13, 2009, all published decisions of the Arkansas Supreme Court and the Arkansas Court of Appeals shall be cited by the case name, by the year of the published decision, by the court abbreviation (Ark. or Ark. App.), and by the appellate decision number, e.g., Whiteside v. Russellville Newspapers, Inc., 2009 Ark. 135 (*In re*: Arkansas Supreme Court and Court of Appeals Rule 5-2, 2009 Ark. 540).

*Bruce L. Plopper*
*Stephen D. Ralph*
*November 2011*
*Conway, Arkansas*

# Chapter 1
# The Arkansas Legal System

Arkansas has a multi-tiered court system, but the lowest courts in this system (those with limited jurisdiction) generally would not handle media-related cases. In November 2000, Arkansans amended the Arkansas Constitution by adopting Amendment 80. This amendment established district courts as the trial courts of limited jurisdiction, subject to the right of appeal to circuit courts. The subject matter of civil cases to be heard by the new district courts is to be established by Arkansas Supreme Court rule, and according to Amendment 80, effective January 1, 2005, the district courts shall be regarded as a continuation of the existing municipal courts, corporation courts, police courts, justice of the peace courts, and courts of common pleas.

Media-related cases tried in the state court system ordinarily would be heard first in circuit courts. According to Amendment 80, circuit courts shall be regarded as a continuation of existing circuit courts, chancery courts, probate courts, and juvenile courts. These courts are headed by elected judges who hear civil and criminal cases.

Litigants wishing to appeal circuit court decisions ask the court of appeals to review non-tort cases (such as those involving questions of obscenity or criminal libel), and they ask the Arkansas Supreme Court to review tort cases (such as those involving questions of privacy or civil libel). The court of appeals consists of 12 elected judges serving eight-year terms. This court may review civil and criminal cases that have been heard in lower courts, and it also may review the decisions of several state-wide commissions.

Judges sitting on the court of appeals are organized into four, three-judge panels, and their decisions must be unanimous for a ruling to stand. When a decision is not unanimous, the case is submitted to a larger panel of six judges, consisting of the original panel plus one other three-judge panel.

The highest state court is the Arkansas Supreme Court. It consists of seven justices, elected for eight-year terms, who may review any lower court decision. This court also has original jurisdiction in several areas.

Amendment 80 also changed the way in which elected judges and justices will run for office. It provided that circuit judges, district judges, court of appeals judges, and supreme court justices shall be elected on a nonpartisan basis, which replaced the system of party affiliation formerly employed.

Although questions concerning interpretation of the First Amendment to the U.S. Constitution may be heard by trial and appellate courts in the Arkansas state court network, plaintiffs in such cases generally would prefer to file their suits in federal court. Exceptions to this preference might include cases involving defamation, obscenity, or other media-related areas in which the state legislature or local governing bodies have codified regulations.

Federal district courts serve as trial courts in the federal court system. As defined by this system, Arkansas is divided into an eastern district, with the main clerk's office in Little Rock, and a western district, with the main clerk's office in Fort Smith. Federal trials, however, are not limited to these two locales, as traveling federal judges hold court in several Arkansas cities, including Fayetteville, Harrison, Jonesboro, Pine Bluff, and Texarkana. Decisions from Arkansas' federal district courts may be appealed to the U.S. Court of Appeals (commonly referred to as the Eighth Circuit), whose jurisdiction consists of federal courts in Arkansas, Iowa, Minnesota, Missouri, Nebraska, North Dakota, and South Dakota.

Ultimately, appeals of Eighth Circuit decisions are taken to the Supreme Court of the United States, which also hears appeals of Arkansas Supreme Court decisions involving interpretations of the U.S. Constitution and of federal statutes.

## Chapter 2

# Freedom of Expression: Theory and Practice

There is no absolute certainty about the Founding Fathers' intentions for the First Amendment's speech and press clause, but from their personal and professional writings, it is clear they did intend to prevent governmental censorship of opinion that criticized political leaders. This did not mean that they would allow all spoken or published thoughts to go unpunished, for the concept of seditious libel was very much alive in the 1790s.

While there are many ways to interpret the First Amendment's protection of speech and press, the most accepted interpretation is that although government generally may not censor communication, it may punish some communicated content. This interpretation is supported by historical research (see, for example, Leonard W. Levy's *Emergence of A Free Press* (1985)) and by a variety of U.S. Supreme Court decisions regarding sedition laws, prior restraint, defamation, invasion of privacy, obscenity, media and the courts, and commercial speech.

Other interpretations have been applied to specific areas of society, rather than gaining the general application of the "no prior restraints" interpretation. For example, the interpretation that political speech (that relating to the self-governing process) and speech concerning well-known individuals (celebrities and other highly visible non-governmental persons) enjoy more protection than other types of speech is seen in U.S. Supreme Court rulings in defamation cases brought by public officials and public figures (New York Times Co. v. Sullivan, 1964; Curtis Publishing Co. v. Butts, 1967).

Another interpretation is that pure speech receives more protection than speech involving action (speech plus). Pure speech refers to the spoken or printed word that is delivered directly to receivers without any accompanying action such as picketing, parading, demonstrating, or soliciting door-to-door. Pure speech generally would be delivered through the mass media or in a public forum, and it is subject to fewer conditions than is speech involving action.

A fourth interpretation is that the First Amendment guarantees speakers a platform from which to speak. This interpretation, though limited in application, has been applied to legally qualified federal political candidates in that during election campaign seasons, they may not be refused time on federally licensed broadcast stations (see the Communications Act of 1934, Sec. 312(a)(7)). It also manifests itself in the rules related to time, place, and manner restrictions that govern public forum use.

One other limited interpretation is that under the First Amendment, the press is special and should be given more freedom than the average person. Though not generally accepted by courts of law, this interpretation recognizes that the news media are the eyes and ears of the public and should be given more access than the general public to places such as accident and disaster scenes, crime scenes, courtrooms, and execution chambers.

Also limited in application is the interpretation that the First Amendment guarantees a right not to speak. This interpretation has been supported in cases where individuals have challenged governmental attempts to force speech, such as when public schools require students to recite the Pledge of Allegiance (West Virginia State Board of Education v. Barnette, 1943) and when state governments require car owners to purchase license plates containing political slogans (Wooley v. Maynard, 1977).

One other interpretation that has gained little traction is the absolutist interpretation. Based upon the idea that "no law means no law," this interpretation is that government has no power to censor or punish pure expression; rather, punishment for harmful expression such as defamation or false advertising should be left to private individuals in their capacity to sue. Former U.S. Supreme Court Justices Hugo Black and William O. Douglas, who served on the Court from the 1930s to the 1970s, were the foremost advocates of this interpretation. They particularly applied this interpretation to obscenity cases.

## The Arkansas Experience

Ever since Arkansas achieved statehood, its Constitution has contained guarantees of free speech and press similar to those in the U.S. Constitution. The state Constitution, however, contains additional provisions that address responsibility for speech and jury considerations for libel.

Article II, Sec. 7 of the 1836 Arkansas Constitution stated,

> "That printing presses shall be free to every person and no law shall ever be made to restrain the rights thereof. The free communication of thoughts and opinions is one of the invaluable rights of man, and every citizen may freely speak, write and print on any subject, being responsible for the abuse of that liberty."

Article II, Sec. 8 of the 1836 Arkansas Constitution stated,

> "In prosecutions for the publication of papers investigating the official conduct of officers or men in public capacity, or where the matter published is proper for public information, the truth thereof may be given in evidence; and in all indictments for libels the jury shall have the right to determine the law and the facts."

Under the title, "Liberty of the press and of speech—Libel," Article II, Sec. 6 of Arkansas' current Constitution (adopted in 1874), freedom of expression also is guaranteed. It reads,

> "The liberty of the press shall forever remain inviolate. The free communication of thoughts and opinions is one of the invaluable rights of man; and all persons may freely write and publish their sentiments on all subjects, being responsible for the abuse of such right. In all criminal prosecutions for libel the truth may be given in evidence to the jury; and, if it shall appear to the jury that the matter charged as libelous is true, and was published with good motives and for justifiable ends, the party charged shall be acquitted."

Despite its heading, language within this section refers only to "liberty of the press," but it clearly retains the cautionary language that such liberty may be abused. The 1874 Constitution also expands the 1836 Constitution's reference to criminal libel, stating that it includes "all criminal prosecutions," rather than merely those involving people "in public capacity" and items "proper for public information."

Although there is occasional discussion about rewriting the Arkansas Constitution, there have been no indications that changes would be made in the expression-related clauses now part of the existing document.

In addition to the free expression provisions of the state Constitution, the Arkansas Criminal Code contains a section on felony slander, which for all intents and purposes makes both the spoken word and the printed word a criminal offense in some situations. This concept is discussed in Chapter 3, "Defamation."

As is evident from a variety of U.S. Supreme Court decisions, the First Amendment is not an absolute protection for free speech and free press. This is typically noted in traditional discussions of free expression theory and practice, which often include references to interpretations and applications of constitutional law.

Several decisions of the Arkansas Supreme Court and the U.S. Court of Appeals for the Eighth Circuit have dealt directly with issues falling into theory and practice categories. These include, for example, topics such as censorship, public forum theory, student expression, and speech-action questions.

## Censorship

The first Arkansas Supreme Court media case that concerned what might be described as "pure censorship" involved the *Arkansas Gazette*, which at the time was one of the state's two widely distributed newspapers (*Arkansas Gazette* v. Lofton, 1980). A trial court had prohibited the newspaper from using the term "Quapaw Quarter rapist" to describe a rape case defendant convicted on two rape charges and facing two more such charges. The high court overturned the trial court's order as an unconstitutional prior restraint.

In 2000, in another case of pure censorship, the Arkansas Supreme Court ruled that the news media could not be prevented from publishing the names or photographs of key figures in an attempted capital murder case (*Arkansas Democrat-Gazette* v. Zimmerman). A county judge had issued such a gag order, which the unanimous court found to be an unconstitutional prior restraint.

A third Arkansas Supreme Court case concerning pure censorship of media involved a 2005 restraining order prohibiting all communication of a witness' testimony in an open court hearing (*Helena Daily World* v. Simes (2006)). The judge overseeing the hearing was accused, by the witness, of judicial misconduct, and a reporter from the newspaper was in attendance and heard the testimony. Shortly after the testimony, the judge closed the hearing and issued the restraining order. This case is discussed more fully in Chapter 7 (Media and Courts).

The Arkansas Supreme Court considered whether publication of the testimony would present a clear and imminent threat to the fair administration of justice. It decided that even though the witness had violated the spirit of the Rules of the Arkansas Judicial and Disability Commission by making public in open court his charges against the presiding judge, the restraining order constituted "… a plain, manifest, clear, and gross abuse of discretion…." (365 Ark. at 312).

In 1988, an Eighth Circuit decision held that several city newsrack ordinances in Des Moines, Iowa, were constitutional time, place, and manner restrictions (Jacobsen v. Crivaro). In this case, the ordinances regulated the size and location of newsracks. The appellate court affirmed the district court opinion and upheld the ordinances because they did not allow city officials to deny newsrack licenses on the basis of content.

A distribution-related issue concerns the legality of posting promotional material and other signs on utility poles. Often, such poles have been used by private individuals to announce such items as garage sales, lost pets, and birthday parties, but Arkansas Code Annotated 5-67-103 (1987) states, "It shall be unlawful for any person, firm, corporation, or association to nail, staple, or otherwise attach or cause to be nailed, stapled, or otherwise attached, any sign, poster, or billboard to any public utility pole or to any living tree, shrub, or other plant located upon the rights-of-way of any public road, highway, or street in this state." While there have been no reported cases involving enforcement of this statute, the U.S. Supreme Court upheld a Los Angeles ordinance that forbid posting signs on public property (Members of City Council v. Taxpayers for Vincent, 1984).

One area of pure censorship recently litigated in Arkansas concerned the rights of nontraditional groups to express themselves in venues afforded to individuals or groups espousing traditional messages. For example, in late 2009, the Arkansas Society of Freethinkers sought permission to erect a "Winter Solstice" display on the State

Capitol grounds, in a location that provided the same prominence as enjoyed by the nativity scene on those same grounds. Arkansas Secretary of State Charlie Daniels denied such permission, and the ASF sued for injunctive relief for violation of its First Amendment rights. According to the complaint, "The purpose of the Winter Solstice display is to provide an expression of some members of the society's beliefs and to provide an opportunity to educate the public about the Winter Solstice and freethinkers." In a Memorandum Opinion and Order filed within four days of the suit's origination, Federal District Court Judge Susan Webber Wright granted the injunction and allowed the ASF to erect its display (The Arkansas Society of Freethinkers v. Charlie Daniels).

A case with similar issues and also decided by Judge Wright originated in 2011, when the United Coalition of Reason, Inc. sued the Central Arkansas Transit Authority and On The Move Advertising, Inc. after the Coalition sought permission to display its message on the sides of 18 city buses serving the city. The message was to read, "Are you good without God? Millions Are." Although the defendants had approved the so-called "bus billboards," they also had required a deposit of up to $36,000 in liability damages, in case those opposed to the message vandalized the buses carrying the message. Judge Wright granted the Coalition's request for a preliminary injunction to allow it to purchase advertising space on the buses at the same rates and on the same terms available to others. She did, however, with minimal explanation, require the Coalition to post a refundable $15,000 bond with the court, in case some vandalism did occur. The preliminary injunction was to remain in place until the case could be heard at a jury trial (United Coalition of Reason, Inc. v. Central Arkansas Transit Authority and On The Move Advertising, Inc.).

Another area of litigation involves punishment for exercising First Amendment rights. One such issue arose in federal district court, but the court refused to rule on it (Wammack v. City of Batesville, 1981). In that case, a former policeman believed that his dismissal occurred because he had exercised his First Amendment rights. The court said that state courts should decide the issue, but to date, there has been no reported decision in this case at the state court level.

Six years later, however, the Eighth Circuit ruled that Southside Public School District of Independence County had unconstitutionally retaliated against three teachers and two administrators because they had exercised their First Amendment Rights (Southside Public Schools v. Hill, 1987). The case arose after the teachers wrote to the Arkansas State Department of Education and complained of delays in implementing programs for disabled students. The trial court also had concluded that the school system was in error. According to trial testimony, representatives of the Southside Public Schools testified that the letter embarrassed administrators, who said they thought it was "... intended to make our school look bad" (p. 272).

Another case involving limits to individual free speech concerned the argument by an attorney that his rights to free speech and association were chilled by the Committee on Professional Conduct, which the Arkansas Supreme Court has designated to regulate the legal profession in Arkansas (Cambiano v. Neal, 2000). The attorney had been disciplined, and the Committee would not allow him to work for or discuss legal matters with other attorneys. The Arkansas Supreme Court affirmed the Conway County Circuit Court's decision, ruling that because the forbidden speech was commercial speech, and because commercial speech garners only intermediate protection under the First Amendment, there was no violation of the attorney's First Amendment rights.

One Arkansas statute that may be considered to be protective of Arkansans' First Amendment rights is the Arkansas Public Employees Political Freedom Act (A.C.A. 21-1-503 (1987)), which protects public employees from being punished for their political activity. Among other things, it protects public employees from retribution for exercising their right to communicate with an elected public official. In the 2011 session of the Arkansas General Assembly, this statute was amended by Act 771, to include protections for public employees' rights and privileges under the Arkansas Freedom of Information Act.

## Public Forum Theory

A public forum is a place or specified area in which members of the public may express themselves with few restrictions. Traditionally, public street corners and sidewalks, school auditoriums (as used for public meetings in earlier times), and public parks served as public forums, but the term has been extended in the past 50 years to include quasi-public places such as shopping malls and specified areas of other privately owned property such as airports and fairgrounds, which generally are used for public purposes.

State and federal courts have recognized that expression in public forums may be regulated by time, place, and manner restrictions that govern when, where, and how public forums may be used. The two guidelines governing such restrictions are that 1) the restrictions must be applied evenhandedly, without regard to the characteristics of the person or persons requesting use, and 2) the restrictions must be content neutral, without regard to the message being communicated. For example, a governmental official issuing permits for use of public streets for parades may neither refuse to issue a parade permit based upon the requestor's religious, social, or political affiliations, nor on whether the requestor's message supports or opposes a given religious, social, or political position; however, a parade permit may be refused if, for example, the parade would interfere with the orderly flow of traffic on a street during rush hour, if noise generated by the parade would disrupt the activities of a school or courtroom, or if the parade would block the entrance to a hospital or other building that generally requires uninterrupted access.

One set of public forum decisions affecting Arkansas concerned policy at the University of Missouri-Kansas City that excluded student religious groups from using university facilities to meet for religious purposes. "Cornerstone," an officially recognized student group, challenged the policy, arguing that content of a group's speech could not be the basis upon which the university could deny a group's use of a public forum. The trial court agreed with the university and issued a summary judgment on its behalf (Chess v. Widmar, 1979). The U. S. Court of Appeals for the Eighth Circuit disagreed, holding that student religious groups have rights equal to those of other groups allowed to meet on campus (Chess v. Widmar, 1980). The university appealed the ruling to the U.S. Supreme Court, which affirmed the Eighth Circuit's decision (Widmar v. Vincent, 1981).

Another public forum issue arose when a former Trans World Airlines employee wanted to protest his firing by standing silently in the Lambert Field (St. Louis) concourse area, with a sign reading, "TWA discriminates against the handicapped" (Jamison v. City of St. Louis, 1987). The employee told the court he believed he had been fired because of his "depression." The airport director denied him permission to protest in this manner, but the Eighth Circuit ruled in the employee's favor. The trial court had ruled that the process by which airport officials had determined who could protest was unconstitutional, but it upheld their right to bar employees from protesting (Jamison v. City of St. Louis, 1986).

The Eighth Circuit found that the airport was a public forum, that the airport director's complete discretion in the matter was an unconstitutional prior restraint, and that the City of St. Louis had not shown how denial of the employee's request furthered the city's interests in either security or operational efficiency.

The most recently reported public forum case began after Arkansas' educational television network excluded a congressional candidate from a televised political debate it had sponsored (Forbes v. Arkansas Educational Television Commission, 1995). Editors at the network felt that to include Ralph P. Forbes, whom they deemed to be a fringe candidate, "... would detract from the debate's usefulness to its intended audience." At trial, a federal jury found that Forbes' rights had not been violated, but the Eighth Circuit reversed, noting that the televised debate was a limited public forum and should have been open to all qualified candidates.

In 1998, the U.S. Supreme Court voted 6-3 in favor of AETN's decision to exclude Forbes from the televised debate (Arkansas Educational Television Commission v. Forbes). Justice Kennedy, writing for the majority, noted that AETN's decision was a reasonable, viewpoint-neutral exercise of journalistic discretion, based upon Forbes' lack of public support. The Court also said the AETN debate was not a public forum.

Within the last 10-15 years, various public universities in Arkansas have established regulations governing public free speech activities (Dungan, 2003). Some designate "free speech zones" on campus, some require advance notice of activities involving large groups, and some govern facilities use by both students and non-students. Although very restrictive campus speech codes may violate the First Amendment, most aspects of existing codes in Arkansas appear to be constitutional time, place, and manner restrictions.

One part of the University of Arkansas at Fayetteville's facilities-use policy, however, was ruled unconstitutional by the Eighth Circuit in April 2006 (Bowman v. White). In part, the policy regulates on-campus speech and literature distribution by non-students. The court found the policy's five-day cap, which limited non-student permits to five, eight-hour days per semester, was not tailored narrowly enough to achieve the university's goal to foster diversity of usage for university facilities. Portions of the policy requiring advance permits and limiting free expression activities on days immediately preceding final exams were upheld.

## Student Expression

In the area of student expression, a 1969 decision by the Eighth Circuit dealt with issues typical of the time (Esteban v. Central Missouri State College). It involved two students who were suspended from the college (now Central Missouri State University) because they violated a college regulation that students must abide by the rules and regulations of the college as well as all local, state, and federal laws. A part of the regulation said, "When a breach of regulations involves a mixed group, ALL MEMBERS ARE HELD EQUALLY RESPONSIBLE."

The suspensions arose after people involved in mass demonstrations blocked a public highway and street, and destroyed school property. The court affirmed the trial court's decision (Esteban v. Central Missouri State College, 1968) and upheld the students' suspension from the college, noting the regulation could be enforced in this way even if the suspended students did not take part in the destructive activities.

A more famous case, which resulted in a 1969 U.S. Supreme Court decision that recognized student free expression rights, began in an Iowa federal district court in 1966 (Tinker v. Des Moines Independent Community School District). At issue was whether the school district could punish students who violated school policy by wearing black armbands in school to protest hostilities in Vietnam. The district court refused to restrain school officials from disciplining students who wore the armbands, the 8th U.S. Circuit Court of Appeals affirmed the decision without opinion, and the U.S. Supreme Court reversed the appellate court's decision.

The Court held that students do not lose their constitutional rights at the schoolhouse gate when they engage in free expression activities that do not invade the rights of others and that do not disrupt the orderly operation of the school. This decision provided the framework under which student expression of all kinds was protected in secondary schools until the *Hazelwood v. Kuhlmeier* (1988) decision (discussed below), but it should be noted that the issue decided in *Tinker* did not involve a school-sponsored activity.

An Arkansas case involving black wristbands worn by students to protest their school's dress code was decided by a federal district court in 2007 (Lowry v. Watson Chapel School District). In an unpublished opinion, the court ruled that the students' First Amendment rights were violated when they were suspended for wearing wristbands on their wrists, forearms, and biceps (erroneously referred to by the district court as armbands) to protest the dress code, but that the dress code itself did not violate the First Amendment because the policy was not intended to prohibit speech. On appeal, the 8th U.S. Circuit Court of Appeals upheld the district court's decision. The school district appealed to the U.S. Supreme Court, but the Court declined to hear the case.

Four years after its *Tinker* decision, the U.S. Supreme Court decided a university free expression case involving a student newspaper editor who also had found little success at the 8th U.S. Circuit Court of Appeals (Papish v. University of Missouri Board of Curators, 1973). In this case, a graduate student was expelled from the university after her independent newspaper, which she sold on campus, ran what university administrators deemed indecent material. In reversing the lower court's decision, the U.S. Supreme Court noted that a university student's First Amendment rights may not be violated merely because that student's expression is offensive to what others believe is good taste.

In 1983, the Eighth Circuit reversed a district court decision and restored a compulsory student fee used to fund the student newspaper at the University of Minnesota (Stanley v. Magrath). The issue was raised after the Board of Regents, following public outcry over a year-end controversial "humor issue," changed the newspaper funding policy to allow students the option of a fee refund.

Students supporting both the newspaper and the former funding policy argued that the Board's new policy violated the editors' First Amendment rights, notwithstanding charges by others that the newspaper had sensationalized religious, social, political, and ethnic groups. The court ruled that the Regents clearly were reacting to the contents of the paper and to the disapproval that others had expressed regarding that content.

Another student expression case grew out of a conflict at a Minnesota high school (Bystrom v. Fridley High School, 1987). Students there wanted to distribute an underground paper on school grounds, without submitting the publication to school administrators for prior review. School regulations stated that no material which was pervasively indecent or vulgar could be distributed on school grounds.

Students argued that prior review was unconstitutional, and that the phrase "pervasively indecent and vulgar" was vague and overbroad. The Eighth Circuit, affirming the trial court's decision, sided with the administration, but it did invalidate another guideline that prohibited material which "invades the privacy of another person or endangers the health or safety of another person." It did so, it said, because Minnesota did not recognize the tort of privacy invasion.

The best-known Eighth Circuit student expression case is *Hazelwood School District v. Kuhlmeier* (1988). The case originated in 1984 in a Missouri Federal District Court, when students sued the district after the school's principal unilaterally deleted two pages of the publication containing stories about teen pregnancy and children of divorced parents.

In 1985, the trial court ruled in favor of the school district, in 1986, the 8th Circuit ruled in favor of the students, and in 1988, the U.S. Supreme Court reversed the Eighth Circuit's decision. In its ruling, the Supreme Court gave broad powers of regulation to school administrators, concerning both school-sponsored newspapers and other school-sponsored activities. It noted that the school's role is to inculcate community values shared by citizens in a civilized society.

As a response to the *Hazelwood* decision, several states enacted student expression laws. Arkansas was the second state within the Eighth Circuit's jurisdiction to do so. During its 1995 session, the Arkansas Legislature passed the Arkansas Student Publications Act (Act 1109), which required each public school board in the state to adopt a written student publications policy by January 1, 1996. The act required school boards to create such policies in conjunction with student publications advisers and appropriate school administrators.

Additionally, it required the policies to recognize that students may exercise their right of expression (including expression in school-sponsored publications) within the framework of the written guidelines. Further, it stipulated that publications policies must recognize that truth, fairness, accuracy, and responsibility are essential to the practice of journalism, and that the following types of publications are not authorized: those that are obscene as to minors; those that are libelous or slanderous; those that constitute unwarranted invasions of privacy; or those that so incite students as to create a clear and present danger of the commission of unlawful acts on school premises or the violation of lawful school regulations, or the material and substantial disruption of the orderly operation of the school.

Another Eighth Circuit decision dealing with student expression occurred in 1999, but this time the expression in question involved election activity (Henerey v. City of St. Charles School District). In this case, a Missouri high school sophomore running for junior class president violated a school board rule when he failed to obtain appropriate permission before handing out condoms as an election technique. Although he won the election, he was disqualified for this oversight. The student argued that other candidates had handed out candy and other traditional electioneering items without obtaining permission, but the Court ruled that the condom distribution in the absence of a public forum interfered with the school's "… legitimate interest in divorcing its extracurricular programs from controversial and sensitive topics, such as teenage sex …" (at 1136).

In May 2000, a Valley View Junior High School student created an Internet site on his home computer, and on the site he criticized some of the school's administrators, staff, and four students (Associated Press, 2000). After discussing the situation with the school's dean of students, the student took down the Internet site and posted an apology, but the student was suspended anyway, during the final exam period. He thus failed ninth grade. In June, after a lawsuit was filed on the student's behalf, a U.S. District Court judge, in an unpublished opinion, ruled that the student should be allowed to take the missed final exams.

Another incident that took place in 2000 involved the expulsion of a Pulaski County Special School District student because of personal compositions he wrote. One of the compositions was taken from the student's home, without the student's knowledge, and was shared with the person about whom it was written (a former girlfriend). Prior to the actual sharing of the composition with the former girlfriend, the student had told the girl that the compositions contained statements about killing her. Ultimately, the student was suspended and later expelled from his school. Through his parents, the student sued the school district. The 8th U.S. Circuit Court of Appeals affirmed the lower court's ruling that the school district terminate the expulsion because the compositions were not true threats and thus were protected speech (Doe v. Pulaski County Special School District, 2001). Both courts took into consideration the fact that the composition was involuntarily shared with the former girlfriend, that the student and his former girlfriend continued to participate peacefully together in church activities, and that the student had personally apologized to the girl and her mother concerning his conduct.

In 2002, however, the 8th Circuit *en banc* overruled the 2001 8th Circuit panel's decision, ruling that the school board did not violate the student's rights when it expelled him because the letter indeed was a true threat 1) because a reasonable recipient would have interpreted it as a serious expression of an intent to harm or cause injury to another, 2) because the letter was communicated to a third party, and 3) because the letter writer testified there was a good possibility the third party would communicate the letter's contents to the intended victim. The court found that in combination, the first two reasons were sufficient to deem the letter a true threat; the third reason merely added to the defendant's difficulty in proving the letter was not a true threat (Doe v. Pulaski County Special School District).

In 2001, the Arkansas Supreme Court decided another student expression case, which involved a student who was suspended for insulting a teacher (Shoemaker v. State). In overruling the lower court's decision, the Arkansas Supreme Court struck down a state statute that made it a misdemeanor for any person to abuse or insult a public school teacher performing normal or assigned school responsibilities. The student, who had uttered the word "bitch" after her teacher repeatedly told her to keep trying to correct an assignment, argued that the statute was unconstitutionally vague. The court agreed, noting that "What language is insulting or abusive is not defined so as to put a reasonable person on notice of the proscribed conduct" (p. 737).

The most recent in-school student expression case began in May 2008, when a high school senior was suspended from the Horatio (Ark.) School District for actions he had taken while speaking at a school event, just prior to graduation. Specifically, the student had played an audio clip from his cell phone, in which a female student said, "Oh my gosh, I'm horny!" The student's cell phone was confiscated, and the student was suspended for three days, which denied him the right to participate in the school's graduation ceremony. In September 2008, the student and his parents filed a complaint against various individuals and the school district, arguing in part that the student's First Amendment rights had been violated. In May 2010, the Arkansas Supreme Court upheld an Arkansas circuit court opinion favoring the school district, noting that the student and his parents had not provided "...any convincing argument or citation to authority on which to reverse" (p. 5). In a dissenting opinion, Justice Brown noted that the plaintiffs had argued nine federal cases to support their position (seven of which were U.S. Supreme Court cases), and that the Arkansas Supreme Court should have decided the free speech portion of the case instead of merely affirming the lower court's opinion (Walters v. Dobbins, Ward, and the Horatio School District).

Whether public school students could be punished for their off-campus, Web-based content became a legal issue in 2004 when two Greenwood (Ark.) High School students were suspended for three days because school administrators decided the students' satirical online comic disrupted the educational process. In February 2005, the *Arkansas Democrat-Gazette* reported that a U.S. District Court judge disagreed and ruled the suspension violated the students' civil rights (Bradford and Rogers, 2005).

This decision may have prompted the 86th Arkansas General Assembly to pass Act 115 in 2007. The new law amends the current law defining anti-bullying policies in public schools and prohibits bullying by an electronic act (cyberbullying) that results in the substantial disruption of the orderly operation of the school or educational environment, whether or not the act originates on school property or with school equipment.

This means that anyone, who through use of such devices as phones or computers, harasses one or more public school students or employees, or creates a substantial disruption of the orderly operation of the school or educational environment, may be guilty of bullying and be punished accordingly.

Coincidentally, the U. S. Supreme Court in 2007 decided a case involving off-campus speech by a high school student in Juneau, Alaska, who was suspended for holding up the sign "BONG HiTS 4 JESUS" at a "Winter Olympics Torch Relay" as the torch passed by his school (Morse v. Frederick). The student was not on school property, and the Ninth U.S. Circuit Court of Appeals had ruled in favor of the student. On appeal, the Court ruled for the school district, finding that the student was attending a school-authorized event and had violated school board policy against any public expression advocating use of substances illegal to minors.

## Speech-Action Questions

Two Arkansas cases from the mid-1950s involved the rights of employees to picket. In the first case, the Arkansas Supreme Court upheld an injunction against peaceful picketing that encouraged employees to break a collective bargaining agreement between a union and the employer's association (Sheet Metal Workers International Ass'n v. E. W. Daniels Plumbing and Heating Co., 1954). The court, focusing its decision on that portion of Article II, Sec. 6 of the Arkansas Constitution which requires citizens to be responsible for the abuse of their free expression rights, said that in some cases, the right to picket was not equal to the right of free speech.

In the second case, union employees picketed to demonstrate that their employer paid sub-standard wages (Self v. Wisener, 1956). The employer, however, claimed that the intent of the picketing was to convince non-union employees to join the union. Citing an absence of statutory law regarding peaceful union picketing, the court sided with the union, saying the judiciary may announce the state's public policy in the matter, in accordance with common law.

## Miscellaneous Issues

Two other expression-related cases from states under the Eighth Circuit's jurisdiction also have reached the federal appellate courts. One of them, an Eighth Circuit case from the mid-1970s, originated when three inmates in the South Dakota Penitentiary were denied permission to receive mail containing sexually explicit material (Carpenter v. State of South Dakota, 1976). The court upheld the ban because it believed the prison censorship board had discretion to decide whether such material could interfere with prisoner rehabilitation. Without a hearing and without requiring a response from the defendants, South Dakota's Federal District Court had dismissed the inmates' petition as frivolous.

Another case, and the only one from Arkansas to reach the U.S. Supreme Court, concerned taxation of publications according to their content (Arkansas Writers' Project v. Ragland, 1987). In this case, publishers of *Arkansas Times*, a general interest magazine, challenged an Arkansas sales tax statute that exempted publications such as newspapers and special interest journals. The Court agreed that the tax was unconstitutional.

# References

## Publications

Associated Press. (2000, July 7). Judge rules for newspaper in FOI lawsuit. *Arkansas Democrat-Gazette*, p. 4B.

Bradford, M., and Rogers, M. (Feb. 23, 2005). Ruling: Students' Web sites protected. *Arkansas Democrat-Gazette*, Northwest Arkansas section, p. 15.

Dungan, T. (2003, July 13). Campuses put limits on speech. *Arkansas Democrat-Gazette*, p. 1B, 7B.

Levy, L. W. (1985). *Emergence of a free press.* New York: Oxford University Press.

## Cases

Arkansas Democrat-Gazette v. Zimmerman, 341 Ark. 771, 20 S.W.3d 301 (2000).

Arkansas Gazette v. Lofton, 269 Ark. 109, 598 S.W.2d 745 (1980).

The Arkansas Society of Freethinkers v. Charlie Daniels, Case Number 4:2009-cv-00925-SWWDocument 9, Dec. 14, 2009.

Arkansas Writers' Project v. Ragland, 481 U.S. 221 (1987).

Bowman v. White, 444 F.3d 967 (8th Cir. 2006).

Bystrom v. Fridley High School, Independent School District No. 14, 822 F.2d 747 (8th Cir. 1987).

Cambiano v. Neal, 342 Ark. 691, 35 S.W.3d 792 (2000).

Carpenter v. State of South Dakota, 536 F.2d 759 (8th Cir. 1976).

Chess v. Widmar, 480 F. Supp. 907 (W.D. Mo. 1979), *affirmed*, 635 F.2d 1310 (8th Cir. 1980), *affirmed*, Widmar v. Vincent, 454 U.S. 263 (1981).

Curtis Publishing Co. v. Butts, 388 U.S. 130 (1967).

Doe v. Pulaski County Special School District, 263 F.3d 833 (8th Cir. 2001), *reversed*, 306 F.3d 616 (8th Cir. 2002).

Esteban v. Central Missouri State College, 290 F. Supp. 622 (W.D. Mo. 1968), *affirmed*, 415 F.2d 1077 (8th Cir. 1969).

Forbes v. Arkansas Educational Television Commission, 93 F.3d 497 (8th Cir. 1995), *affirmed,* 523 U.S. 666 (1998).

Frederick v. Morse, 439 F.3d 1114 (9th Cir. 2006), *reversed*, Morse v. Frederick, 551 U.S. 393 (2007).

Hazelwood School District v. Kuhlmeier, 484 U.S. 260 (1988).

Helena Daily World v. Simes, 365 Ark. 305 (2006).

Henerey v. City of St. Charles School District, 200 F.3d 1128 (8th Cir. 1999).

Jacobsen v. Crivaro, 851 F.2d 1067 (8th Cir. 1988).

Jamison v. City of St. Louis, 671 F. Supp. 641 (E.D. Mo. 1986), *affirmed*, 828 F.2d 1280 (8th Cir. 1987).

Lowry v. Watson Chapel School District, Case No. 5:06CV00262 JLH (E.D. Ark. October 12, 2007), *affirmed*, 540 F.3d 752 (8th Cir. 2008), *cert. denied*, 129 S. Ct. 1526 (2009).

Members of City Council v. Taxpayers for Vincent, 466 U.S. 789 (1984).

New York Times Co. v. Sullivan, 376 U.S. 254 (1964).

Self v. Wisener, 226 Ark. 58, 287 S.W.2d 890 (1956).

Sheet Metal Workers International Ass'n, Local No. 249 v. E. W. Daniels Plumbing & Heating Co., Inc., 223 Ark. 48, 264 S.W.2d 597 (1954).

Shoemaker v. State, 343 Ark. 727, 38 S.W.3d 350 (2001).

Southside Public Schools v. Hill, 827 F.2d 270 (8th Cir. 1987).

Stanley v. Magrath, 719 F.2d 279 (8th Cir. 1983).

United Coalition of Reason, Inc. v. Central Arkansas Transit Authority and On The Move Advertising, Inc., Case Number 4:2011-cv-00450, Aug. 16, 2011.

Walters v. Dobbins, Ward, and the Horatio School District, 2010 Ark. 260.

West Virginia State Board of Education v Barnette, 319 U.S. 624 (1943).

Wammack v. City of Batesville, 522 F. Supp. 1006 (E.D. Ark. 1981).

West Virginia State Board of Education v. Barnette, 319 U.S. 624 (1943).

Wooley v Maynard, 430 U.S. 705 (1977).

## Constitutions and Statutes

Arkansas Constitution, Article II, Section 7 (1836).

Arkansas Constitution, Article II, Section 8 (1836).

Arkansas Constitution, Article II, Section 6 (1874).

Arkansas Public Employees Political Freedom Act, A.C.A. 21-1-503 (1987).

Arkansas Student Publications Act, A.C.A. 6-18-1201 *et seq*. (1987).

Communications Act of 1934, political access policy, 47 U.S.C. §312(a)(7)(2006).

School Districts (Bullying), A.C.A. 6-18-514(a) (1987).

Chapter 3

# Defamation

Historically, defamation cases have caused the media more nuisance than cases of any other kind, and this has been especially true in modern times. The relatively large number of such cases in Arkansas stems primarily from common law, although the state has some statutes governing both criminal and civil actions for defamation.

Criminal defamation, which in Arkansas technically is slander that is spoken or published, is codified in Arkansas Code Annotated 5-15-101 *et seq.* (1987), which contains thorough definitions of this felony. The law also designates the statute of limitations deadline (one year) and penalties (imprisonment in the penitentiary from between six months to three years or a fine of between $50-3,000, or both). The criminal slander statute also states that nothing in the law shall be construed to prevent any person slandered from bringing and maintaining a civil suit for damages against any person committing the slander.

Civil defamation is not defined by statute, but Arkansas Code Annotated 16-56-104 to 16-56-105 (1987) defines the statute of limitations deadline as one year for civil slander and three years for civil libel. Additionally, Arkansas Code annotated 16-63-207 (1987) contains language governing statements for a cause of action, as well as language concerning truth as a defense and mitigating circumstances as a way to reduce the amount of damages. For civil defamation, Arkansas Code Annotated 16-62-101 (1987) states that under common law, action for slander abates with the death of either party. The Arkansas Supreme Court, however, in 1992 ruled that tortious injury to a person survives the death of the person causing the injury (the tort-feasor), and that action for such injury may be brought against the estate or personal representative of the tort-feasor in cases not involving libel or slander (Westridge v. Byrd).

Defamation in political broadcasts is covered in Arkansas code Annotated 7-6-104 (1987), which states that where Congress or the Federal Communications Commission prohibits broadcasters from censoring the script, broadcasters have no liability for any defamatory statement uttered as part of a broadcast by candidates for political office.

It has clearly been established that libel or slander consists of several elements, all of which must be present in most situations for a plaintiff to have a successful cause of action. These elements are 1) defamatory content that causes harm, 2) publication, 3) identification, 4) fault, and 5) falsity. In civil cases, the question of damages also arises, but the Arkansas Supreme Court has ruled that to collect damages, proof of harm to reputation must be shown (United Insurance Co. of America v. Murphy, 1998).

## Defamation Defined

Criminal defamation (slander) in Arkansas is defined in a variety of ways, but the definitions make it clear that to win criminal slander cases, the words in question must be false and plaintiffs may not attach esoteric meanings to them. The felony slander statute specifies three categories of falsehoods as offenses, and these are 1) charging fornication or adultery, 2) charging false swearing, and 3) proclaiming one as a coward for not accepting a challenge.

Also, the statute contains a "catch-all" section that additionally defines slander as falsely using, uttering, or publishing words which, in their common acceptation, charge a person with having been guilty of any other crime or misdemeanor not specified in the above-mentioned three categories; charge any person with having been guilty of any dishonest business or official conduct or transaction, the effect of which charge would be to injure the person's credit or business standing; or bring into disrepute the good name or character of such person so slandered.

Although the U.S. Supreme Court has made it very difficult for public officials to win criminal slander cases, a criminal slander case brought by a governmental employee who is not a public official may survive a constitutional challenge. Such employees would be people who do not have, or are not perceived by the public as having, power over governmental policy or finances, and people who, in their roles as governmental employees, do not thrust themselves into the public spotlight.

In both criminal and civil defamation, statutory language allows that truth may be offered in evidence as a defense. It may be recalled that Article II, Sec. 6 of the Arkansas Constitution supports truth as a defense in criminal prosecutions for libel, although the "truth" referred to there must have been published with good motives and justifiable ends (this language seems to conflict with the holdings of many court decisions that allow truth as an absolute defense in libel cases, regardless of motives or intended result). Only statutory language concerning civil libel and slander, however, allows mitigating circumstances to be introduced to reduce the amount of damages.

Additionally, the Arkansas Supreme Court's reasoning in two non-media defamation cases clarified the meaning of defamatory language. In an oft-quoted case, the court said defamation had occurred because "... words were spoken and published with the malicious intent of impeaching appellee's honesty, integrity, veracity and reputation, and exposed him to public hate, contempt, and ridicule ...." (Sinclair Refining Co. v. Fuller, 1935). In a more recent case, the court noted that under Arkansas law, even if a crime is not directly charged, slander may occur if a crime is imputed (Goodman v. Phillips, 1951).

It is common to classify libel and slander as *per se* or *per quod*. Libel or slander *per se* means that the defamation flows directly from the words used, and that anyone applying common meanings to the words would know that they could harm a person's reputation. For example, calling someone a liar or cheat, if untrue, could be libel *per se*.

On the other hand, libel or slander *per quod* means that the people seeing or hearing the statement in question would have to know additional information about the situation for the statement to be considered defamatory. For example, a photo caption identifying Todd Jones taking part in a pro-abortion rally may not appear to be defamatory. But suppose Todd is the leader of a local anti-abortion group, and he was just passing by the pro-abortion rally when his picture was taken. The incorrect photo caption might change some people's opinions of Todd and in their eyes ruin his reputation as an abortion foe.

An analysis of the defamation element in Arkansas media law

cases identifies the types of words and phrases litigated as alleged defamation and also provides historical background concerning libel and slander.

The first Arkansas Supreme Court decision concerning libel involved a newspaper advertisement in which one person said another person was a swindler (Obaugh v. Finn, 1842). In the early 1900s, the editor of the *Morrilton Democrat* was accused of defaming the town's mayor after the editor suggested in writing that the mayor might "... backbite his friends and lay down with his enemies ... tell secrets out of the lodge ..." and "... change friends and issues upon very short order" (Patton v. Cruce, 1904).

In 1907, the Arkansas Supreme Court said, "In ascertaining the meaning of words, spoken or written, to determine whether or not they are libelous, the entire conversation or writing must be considered" (Miller v. State). The occasion was a criminal libel suit against the editor of the *Argenta Daily News* of North Little Rock, in which the headline "Bob Rogers Offers a Bribe and Then Commits Forgery" was at issue. The court reiterated this stance in 1912 when it reviewed a suit brought by a census-taker who was the object of the following line in a newspaper article: "A man's motive is no excuse for his stealing" (Skaggs v. Johnson).

In 1915, the court ruled that an article in the *Luxora Commonwealth* (Mississippi County) contained words that were libelous *per se* (Simonson v. Lovewell). The article accused the sheriff, who was up for re-election, of "… squandering and appropriating to his own uses ... thousands of dollars of the people's money ..." (p. 85, 408).

Two years later, the Arkansas Supreme Court heard a case involving two stories in the *Morrilton Democrat* (Bloodworth v. Times Publishing Co., 1917). One story involved publication of "The Knocker's Prayer," which was supposed to reflect sentiments of people opposed to progress and growth for a town. It contained language indicating that knockers lie, would steal if they had the courage, and would try to put businesses out of business. The other story identified the plaintiff as a knocker, which he said linked him to "The Knocker's Prayer." The court agreed.

In 1922, in a case involving an article in the *McRae Progress*, the court found no libel of business owners by a disgruntled former partner who described his dealings with those bringing the libel suit

(Honea v. King). The court said words must be taken in context and at their most natural and obvious meaning.

Two Arkansas Supreme Court decisions in the 1940s also helped to identify the boundaries of libelous language. In one, the contents of a letter published in the *Daily Times Echo* of Eureka Springs were found to be libelous *per se* because the contents charged a husband and wife team with using underhanded methods, discriminating statements, and pure falsehoods to turn away prospective patients from a hospital owned by the defendant (Baker v. State, 1940). The two accused of these actions became prosecution witnesses for the state in a criminal libel trial.

The other media case decided in this decade was brought because of editorials in the *West Memphis News* (West Memphis News v. Bond, 1947). During a primary election campaign, the newspaper charged that a county judge nominee was the leader of a corrupt remnant of a county gang. In part, the editorials said, "You and your gang got rich allowing gambling dens and brothels to operate openly, ... by cheating ignorant negroes, and (through) various other grafts" (p. 517, 451).

Although this language was found to be defamatory, a different outcome may have occurred had the case been heard after the U.S. Supreme Court decided *New York Times Co. v. Sullivan* (1964). In that case, the Court created breathing room for robust, wide-open debate about issues of public importance, a category into which county elections surely would fall. In short, the Court held that in such instances, libel could be found only if it was published with "actual malice," which it defined as knowing falsehood or reckless disregard of truth.

Language found to be defamatory in a 1952 case involving the *Arkansas State Press*, however, probably would not have enjoyed Constitutional protection after *New York Times Co. v. Sullivan* (State Press Co. v. Willett). The case was brought by a black clergyman named Willett, who had been criticized by the newspaper for the views he offered on his weekly radio program. The paper said, "His white supporters ... show very poor judgment in their selection of Willett's type to vilify the Negro. There are many men known to the White man, and the Negro, who will vilify the Negro for a price with a certain amount of dignity" (p. 852, 404). The Arkansas Supreme Court upheld the trial court's judgment of $100 compensatory damages and

$1,400 in punitive damages because, it said, the paper made no attempt to prove any arrangement between Rev. Willett and his sponsors, by which, according to the newspaper, he was to be paid to vilify his race.

None of the three media-related libel cases that dealt with types of defamatory language and were heard by the Arkansas Supreme Court in the 1960s went against the media. The first two, decided early in the decade, involved accurate reports of information that, despite their truthfulness, may have been harmful to the reputations of those described. One concerned a report in *The Eagle Democrat* of Warren, Ark., which said a lawyer had used a legal technicality to send an admitted criminal to the state hospital for observation (Roberts v. Love, 1960). The lawyer charged that the newspaper had conveyed the impression that he was insincere in his defense, and that he had endeavored to defeat justice by trickery. The other case involved publication of a person's name in a debt collection agency's credit information bulletin (Reese v. Haywood, 1962).

The third case was brought as the result of an article and an editorial in the *Morrilton Democrat*, in which the former reported on two lawsuits challenging ballot results, and the latter criticized elections in Conway County and poked fun at one contested election in particular (Wirges v. Brewer, 1965). The Conway County clerk, who was responsible for the absentee ballots referred to in the editorial, brought suit. Noting that neither the clerk nor his office had been mentioned in the editorial, the Arkansas Supreme Court ruled that extrinsic evidence could not serve to enlarge the language of a published article or editorial that contained no charge of corruption or wrongdoing.

The two Arkansas Supreme Court media libel cases that helped define defamation in Arkansas ended in decisions supporting the media. The first involved an unsigned letter to the editor, complaining that the police in Crossett, Ark., among other things, did not like boys with long hair (Pigg v. Ashley County Newspaper, Inc., 1973). The author of the letter said he wasn't going to buy anything from Crossett merchants until one specific officer was fired from the force. The named officer sued, but he lost his case because the court believed no libel existed when contents of the entire letter were considered.

In a 1982 case, KFSM-TV in Fort Smith won its case against a sheriff who believed he had been libeled by the station's report of a

Grand Jury investigation of the sheriff's office (Pritchard v. Times Southwest Broadcasting, Inc.). The report contained references to two matters not being considered by the Grand Jury, and the sheriff argued that because the matters were mentioned, viewers would think the Grand Jury was investigating them. He believed the report intended to convey false information that the reporter knew to be false, but the court found neither the intent nor the implication that the sheriff tried to prove.

Another 1980s case involving a television station went against the media at the trial level (KARK-TV v. Simon, 1983). In this instance, KARK-TV in Little Rock reported an attempted robbery involving hostage-taking and showed scenes of the police clearly placing the plaintiffs in a squad car. As it turned out, there was no robbery attempt, no hostage-taking, and no arrests. After the Arkansas Supreme Court reversed and remanded the decision on grounds that punitive damages should not have been awarded, the case was settled out of court.

In early 1991, a defamation case that received national publicity was filed by Oliver Miller, a University of Arkansas basketball player, against the company that owned two television stations in the Rogers/Fort Smith area (Miller v. J.D.G. Television, Inc.). The case arose after the television stations linked the basketball player to a sexual assault incident. The player denied participating in the incident, and in his complaint, stated that he had not been contacted by the stations prior to their reports about the incident, that by the time of one broadcast he had been cleared of any wrongdoing, and that the broadcasts regarding his alleged involvement in the incident were not based on a credible, reliable source. This case, too, was settled out of court.

Later that year, a Federal District Court jury in Arkansas awarded $1.5 million in damages to a 96-year-old Arkansas resident who had sued a tabloid newspaper for using her picture to illustrate one of its stories (Mitchell v. Globe International Publishing, Inc.). The award was later reduced to $1.1 million. In addition to the defamation claim, the plaintiff sued for false light invasion of privacy and for emotional distress.

The story was about a 101-year-old grandmother who finally had to give up her paper route because she had become pregnant. The tabloid, which had used a pseudonym for the woman, argued that its editors thought the woman was dead and that because what the tabloid printed was basically fiction anyway, few readers would take its contents as truth. The jury rejected the defamation claim, but it awarded damages for the privacy and emotional distress claims. In early 1992, the presiding judge upheld the jury's decision, and the following year, the U.S. Supreme Court, without comment, let the district court's decision stand.

Other potentially defamatory words were the basis of litigation in 1993, after the specialty publication *Arkansas Business* published comments of one person about another (Waymire v. DeHaven). The comments were made by Jay DeHaven, who said Richard Waymire "is an absolute con" and "He's an absolute crook." The trial court judge granted summary judgment because he thought the statements weren't slander *per se*, but the Arkansas Supreme Court reversed and remanded, noting that the words were reasonably capable of a particular interpretation, and that a jury must decide if the words were in fact so understood.

In 1997, the Arkansas Supreme Court ruled that the *Arkansas Democrat-Gazette* defamed a former U.S. attorney when it mistakenly published his picture in conjunction with a story about a federal Whitewater case defendant with the same last name (Little Rock Newspapers, Inc. v. Fitzhugh). The court said Fitzhugh was a private person, for the purposes of the law suit, and thus needed to prove only negligence, rather than actual malice. In 1998, the U.S. Supreme Court declined to hear the case.

Another aspect of defamation that has arisen in Arkansas concerns the differentiation between fact and opinion in an alleged defamatory communication. Citing a 1986 Eighth Circuit decision (Janklow v. Newsweek, Inc.), the Arkansas Supreme Court in *Bland v. Verser* (1989) adopted a four-part test to determine whether remarks are opinions or facts. Part one deals with the precision and specificity of the disputed remarks (it is difficult to call a vague or imprecise statement a "fact"); part two concerns verifiability of the remarks (if a statement cannot plausibly be verified, it cannot be seen as "fact"); part three denotes the "literary context" in which the remarks were made (statements must be taken as part of a whole, including tone and the use of cautionary language); and part four considers the "public context" in which the remarks were made (statements made in a public or political arena receive more protection).

## Publication

For the purposes of defamation suits, publication generally means communication of information to a third party. As recently as 2003, the Arkansas Court of Appeals confirmed that "... 'publication' occurs when the defamatory matter is communicated to someone other than the person defamed" (Northport Health Services, Inc. v. Owens, 82 Ark. App. at 361, 107 S.W.3d at 892). This may be accomplished in any number of ways, including through the printed word, verbalizations, photographs, or drawings.

Although sharing information with just one other person often satisfies the requirement of publication, the Arkansas Supreme Court has recognized occasions in which such sharing is considered privileged and not subject to successful defamation suits. The court's earliest recognition of such privilege, as applied to defamation, came in a 1911 non-media case involving a report by a life insurance investigation company (Bohlinger v. Germania Life Insurance Co.). In establishing conditional privilege in defamation actions, the court said, "A communication is held to be qualifiedly privileged when it is made in good faith upon any subject-matter in which the person making the communication has an interest, or in reference to which he has a duty, and to a person having a corresponding interest or duty, although it contains matter which, without such privilege, would be actionable" (pp. 482-83, 259).

The court embraced this position again in 1981 in a non-media case involving a doctor who allegedly defamed a nurse (Farris v. Tvedten), and in 1989 in a non-media case involving corporation executives (Navorro-Monzo v. Hughes). In the former case, two others saw the statement in question: one person was the doctor's stenographer who typed the letter containing the statement, and the other person was the nurse's spouse. The court said qualified privilege existed between the doctor and his stenographer, and that the doctor was not responsible for actions beyond his control, i.e., the nurse sharing the statement with her husband.

In the latter case, which involved statements about a restaurant manager's handling of funds, the court found qualified privilege to exist between a corporation's president and its board of directors.

In a 1978 Eighth Circuit decision, however, the court of appeals said the Arkansas Supreme Court probably would hold defendants liable for unauthorized republications of a libel, if such republications were reasonably foreseeable (Luster v. Retail Credit Company). This case involved a retail credit company report that in so many words led readers to believe an employer had torched his own business. The difference between the credit report case and the above-noted doctor/nurse case is that the credit report case involved a much more public situation and was more likely to be the subject of media republication. That a letter may be shared with a spouse is foreseeable, but it clearly is not the type of damaging republication the Eighth Circuit had in mind.

Another limitation to qualified privilege was noted by the Arkansas Supreme Court in a 2002 case involving claims of defamation, intrusion, and false light invasion of privacy (Wal-Mart Stores, Inc. v. Lee). In this case, the court noted that if the author of an allegedly defamatory statement does not believe it is true, then the statement is not protected by a qualified privilege.

The Arkansas Supreme Court also has ruled on the republication issue concerning reports of judicial proceedings (Jones v. Commercial Printing Co., 1971). The issue arose when the *Pine Bluff Commercial* reported an attorney's legal action to inspect bank records; the attorney thought the reports attacked his integrity. After the attorney filed his libel suit, the newspaper both reported the libel suit filing and printed an answer to the charges in the filing. The attorney then tried to introduce that story as a republication of the original libel, trying to show aggravation of damages. While the court said he should be allowed to introduce such evidence, it also ruled that the report of a judicial proceeding is privileged if it is complete, impartial, and accurate.

One republication issue that has not been heard by the Arkansas Supreme Court since the early 1900s has to do with timing. The court in 1908 ruled that republication of a libel cannot be a cause of action if it occurs prior to legal action on the original publication (Murray v. Galbraith). This holding differs from the modern holdings of other courts, and it may be overruled if it comes to the Arkansas Supreme Court again.

Courts have recently been asked to consider whether Internet service providers (ISPs) may be held liable as publishers of defamatory communications posted upon Web sites. This issue may be of particular concern for news organizations that maintain separate Web sites for public information and for public interaction with a news service. In 1996, Congress passed as part of the Communications Decency Act a provision, §230, which immunizes an ISP from liability as a "publisher," so long as it does not originate the defamatory material.

In a recent decision of first impression in its jurisdiction, the Eighth Circuit held a Web site host, ComplaintsBoard.com, not liable for posting apparent defamatory statements that an operator of a cat breeding business, Cozy Kittens Cattery, "kill(s) cats," "rip(s) off cat breeders," and "steal(s) kittens." The Court observed that the framework of the federal law was intended to "bar plaintiffs from holding ISPs legally responsible for information that third parties created and developed" (Johnson v. Arden, 2010). The decision specifically notes that the federal law preempts any state law to the contrary.

## Identification

Generally, the element of identification involves information allowing a third party to link a recognizable person or small group to a defamatory statement. This includes but is not limited to names, addresses, physical descriptions, relational descriptions, and unique personal habits. While care should be taken not to falsely implicate identifiable individuals when discussing character faults or issues of wrongdoing, it is important to include full identification (including middle initials) of people mentioned in news stories about specific wrongdoing. When such identification is missing, others with similar names may sue successfully for defamation if they can prove that readers would be confused concerning who exactly has been linked to such wrongdoing.

The first Arkansas Supreme Court media case involving identification was decided in 1908, after the *Morrilton Democrat* published a piece that condemned "wine joints" (Comes v. Cruce). The piece was prompted by the killing of a white man by one or more members of a minority group, and it contained the following passage: "The killing near the river Saturday evening was the result of the wine joints now in operation here ... it is the general opinion, even of those who use the wine, that it is adulterated, and much of it possibly never saw a grape" (pp. 80-81, 186). One person who ran a winery sued for libel, but the court held that the article referred only to a class of people rather than to individuals.

Fifty years later, the court decided an identification question in a non-media case with media-related applications (Thiel v. Dove, 1958). The case was brought against a municipal judge in Paragould who told people that as he stood on a sidewalk and looked into an apartment building window, he had seen enough to know that a city policeman had had sex with a woman in the apartment. He didn't identify the woman, but she and her husband lived alone in the apartment the judge identified. The woman sued for slander and won, and even though the Arkansas Supreme Court reversed the lower court's decision because of faulty jury instructions, the high court accepted the plaintiff's identification argument.

## Fault

In any successful defamation case, a plaintiff must establish fault on the part of the defendant. This means that in cases involving private parties, the plaintiff must prove at least ordinary negligence, defined in Arkansas as a deviation from the standard of care that a reasonably prudent person would observe in the same or similar circumstances. Public figures or public officials who bring defamation suits concerning statements related to their public activities must prove "actual malice," which the U.S. Supreme Court has defined as either reckless disregard of truth or knowing falsehood (New York Times Co. v. Sullivan, 1964).

As mentioned above, the concept of privilege also comes into play in discussions of fault, and for the media, this is an important issue. Fair, accurate, and impartial media reports of most governmental proceedings and statements made by officials in their official capacities, despite content that is false and defamatory, are not actionable because the media have qualified privilege to publish such information.

One incident in which privileged information resulted in legal action involved the *Arkansas Gazette*, which published an Arkansas governor's statement about nursing home irregularities and included a description of conditions at one particular nursing home (Brandon v. Gazette Publishing Company, 1961). The primary owner of the nursing home sued, but the Arkansas Supreme Court found the *Gazette* story to be conditionally privileged.

Another 1961 Arkansas Supreme Court case arose after a Dun & Bradstreet newsletter reported to 36 subscribers that a local wholesaler had discontinued service (Dun & Bradstreet, Inc. v. Robinson). The information had been obtained from another business in the same town, but it had not been checked. A few days later, when it was checked and found to be wrong, a correction was issued, but because of the earlier negligence, the jury found for the plaintiff. The verdict was upheld on appeal.

Four years later, another Dun & Bradstreet case reached the Eighth Circuit Court of Appeals (Dun & Bradstreet, Inc. v. Nicklaus, 1965). It also involved an erroneous report about a business, but because the report had neither been checked by the newsletter correspondent who filed it nor reviewed by anyone in authority, the appellate court upheld a verdict based upon reckless disregard of truth. Even though Dun & Bradstreet had attempted to correct its mistake in a subsequent publication, the court found that the correction was not complete enough to overcome the earlier incompetence.

Four media-related cases that reached the Arkansas Supreme Court in the 1970s dealt with the "actual malice" fault standard. The first, decided in 1973, was brought against the *Arkansas Gazette* by an assistant dean at the University of Arkansas law school (Gallman v. Carnes). The newspaper had published an article critical of the assistant dean, and although the article was based upon documents prepared by the law school's committee on faculty tenure and promotion, the assistant dean claimed it fashioned a direct attack on his qualifications as a professor and legal scholar. The court ruled that the assistant dean was a public official and that no actual malice had been shown.

The second case resulted in the court's declaration that Arkansas' criminal libel statute was unconstitutional because, among other faults, it did not allow truth as a defense and it did not require the *New York Times Co. v. Sullivan* actual malice standard (Weston v. State, 1975). The case arose after an editorial in the *Sharp Citizen* (Sharp County) accused a deceased resident of owning a still while he was alive. This is a felony in Arkansas, and the Arkansas statute in force at the time allowed, in part, for criminal libel actions to brought against those who, through malicious defamations, blackened the memory of the dead. In 1975, the Arkansas General Assembly passed a revised criminal libel statute.

In 1978, another case involving actual malice reached the court (Saxton v. Arkansas Gazette Co.). It arose after the *Arkansas Gazette* published an article noting that minutes of an Arkansas Soil and Water Conservation Commission meeting didn't exactly reflect what was said at the meeting. The executive director of the commission, who was responsible for the minutes, sued, claiming he had been accused of falsifying the minutes. The court ruled that because the executive director was a public official, actual malice had to be shown. The court found no actual malice on the part of the reporter.

The final 1970s media-related case involving the actual malice standard was decided in 1979, after an attorney sued the *Arkansas Democrat* because a story it ran stated that the attorney had failed the bar exam (Dodrill v. *Arkansas Democrat*). The attorney's name had been left off the official list of those who had passed the exam, so the newspaper's assumption was that he had failed it. This was not the case. The court ruled that the attorney was not a public figure and was therefore required to prove only negligence on the part of the newspaper. In a dissenting opinion, however, three justices argued that the attorney was a limited public figure because his license to hold a position of public trust was at issue.

In the 1980s, four cases involved Arkansas Supreme Court distinctions between negligence and actual malice. Two 1981 cases provided insight into judicial thinking on this topic. The first involved an erroneous report in the *Arkansas Democrat*, concerning the type of license a tavern had received (Wortham v. Little Rock Newspapers, Inc.). The court granted summary judgment for the newspaper because no actual malice was shown, but the dissenting opinion addressed an important issue. That opinion criticized the majority's case-by-case approach and argued for a stronger First Amendment prohibition against granting damages for errors committed during discussions of public affairs.

The other 1981 case involved Magnolia's local newspaper, *The Daily Banner-News*, which had run a series of 11 editorials critical of city police and certain police officers (Lancaster v. The Daily Banner-News Publishing Co., Inc.). The court found no actual malice, noting that failure of the newspaper to investigate charges against the police did not amount to the high degree of awareness of probable falsity demanded by the U.S. Supreme Court's actual malice standard.

Public officials were involved in two 1987 cases concerning the actual malice fault standard. In one, a Pulaski County deputy sheriff appealed a summary judgment order favoring the *Arkansas Demo-*

*crat*, which had reported on the activity surrounding the deputy sheriff's dismissal from the Pulaski County sheriff's Department (Hollowell v. Arkansas Democrat Newspaper). The court ruled that the deputy sheriff did not meet the required actual malice standard.

In the second case, the chairman of the board of governors of Chicot County Memorial Hospital had sued Little Rock broadcast station KATV-TV for reporting erroneously that he had been charged with a felony rather than with a misdemeanor (Drew v. KATV Television, Inc.). The court upheld a summary judgment favoring the television station, finding that there had been no showing of actual malice.

A much-publicized non-media case involving the fault standard in defamation concerned a politician and his opponent's political consultant (Fuller v. Russell, 1992). In this case, a lower court had found that a candidate for the Arkansas General Assembly had libeled his opponent's political consultant because in a letter to about 500 voters, the candidate had called the consultant "Mr. Negative" and a "negative tactician." The Arkansas Supreme Court, agreeing with candidate Ron Fuller that the consultant, Jerry L. Russell, was a limited public figure who had not provided clear and convincing evidence of actual malice, reversed the lower court's decision.

The Fuller court also noted that "...reckless conduct is not measured by whether a reasonably prudent man would have published, or would have investigated before publishing. There must be sufficient evidence to permit the conclusion that the defendant in fact entertained serious doubts as to the truth of his publication. Publishing such doubts shows reckless disregard for truth or falsity and demonstrates actual malice" (311 Ark. at 108, 842 S.W.2d at 14).

Most recently, Fayetteville mayoral candidate Dan Coody sued Thomson Newspapers and a former publisher for libel after the *Northwest Arkansas Times* ran a 1992 pre-election editorial and a story that reflected on Coody's qualifications for office (Thomson Newspaper Publishing, Inc. v. Coody, 1995). Despite testimony that the editorial contained false information, testimony from the paper's employees at the time that the publisher at the time was hostile toward Coody's candidacy, and testimony that the publisher may not have checked his facts with sources until after the items were published, the Arkansas Supreme Court reversed the trial court's $275,000 judgment for Coody. The court said there was no evidence that the publisher was aware of the falsity of the material in the editorial, there was no proof that the publisher entertained serious doubts as to the truth of his publication, and that although ill will had been established, Coody had not provided clear and convincing evidence of actual malice.

In late 1995, the U.S. Supreme Court declined to hear the Coody case, but in 1996, the new executive editor of the *Northwest Arkansas Times* published a full-page apology to Coody (Lancaster, 1996). The apology said, "I believe, as do others here, that the *Northwest Arkansas Times* fell well short of journalistic standards during Fayetteville's mayoral campaign of 1992. Our newspaper, then under different ownership and management, helped facilitate and circulate unfounded questions in a vicious rumor campaign against a candidate named Dan Coody."

One other case relevant to the fault question was decided in 1985 by the Federal District Court serving the eastern district of Arkansas (Lemmer v. Arkansas Gazette Company). In this case, a former member of an organization named Vietnam Veterans Against the War sued the *Arkansas Gazette* after it ran a story that said he had played a major role in helping the FBI crush the organization through false accusations and interference. The court ruled that due to his high visibility concerning this issue, the plaintiff was a public figure. The newspaper won the case because there was no showing of actual malice.

An issue concerning the fair-report privilege was raised in a 2009 Arkansas Supreme Court defamation case brought by Ryan Whiteside against the *Russellville Courier* after the newspaper published what Whiteside characterized as untruths and falsehoods concerning his integrity and character. The case arose after the newspaper published several stories about an alleged rape that supposedly had occurred at Whiteside's house and supposedly had involved Whiteside at some point.

Further, Whiteside complained that the newspaper had obtained information for its story from a statewide computer system (AEGIS) used by law enforcement agencies and that such information should not be considered part of official documents subject to the fair-report privilege. Whiteside also argued that the newspaper lost its fair-report privilege because the articles did not constitute a fair and accurate report. The court disagreed on all counts and affirmed the Pope County Circuit Court's decision favoring the newspaper (Whiteside v. Russellville Newspapers, Inc.).

## Falsity

To constitute libel or slander, the statements in question must be false, for truth is an absolute defense against defamation charges. Of course, not all false statements that injure a person's reputation are legally actionable. As noted above, the reporting of some false statements are qualifiedly privileged; also, for erroneous statements about public figures or public officials to be actionable, they must either be knowing falsehoods or be made with reckless disregard for truth. Many cases discussed in the preceding sections of this chapter illustrate types of falsities that prompt defamation suits against the media and types of falsities the media cannot legally justify.

## Damages

In civil suits involving defamation, plaintiff may ask for a variety of monetary damages. Nominal damages may be awarded in suits where the plaintiff wins but has suffered only negligible harm. Nominal damages are symbolic and are awarded mostly for loss of honor or as a moral victory.

Presumed damages used to be awarded upon a showing of defamation, without proof of loss, as it was presumed that a plaintiff had been damaged by the act itself. Courts today, including those in Arkansas, have moved away from arbitrarily awarding presumed damages.

The two types of compensatory damages are general and special. General damages, also known as actual damages, are awarded for unquestionable loss of reputation and other non-measureable elements such as pain and emotional distress. Special damages are awarded for measureable out-of-pocket expenses or losses, such as bills for hospital care and other medical care, loss of business, and loss of contributions.

Punitive damages are awarded both to punish the defendant and to make an example of the defendant, so others will not imitate the defendant's behavior. These damages often include large sums of money and also are known as exemplary damages and as "smart-money" damages.

The Arkansas Court of Appeals in 2003 noted it followed a two-step process to determine whether punitive damages were excessive (Superior Federal Bank v. Mackey). The first step is to review the award under state law, which "… entails an analysis of whether the jury's verdict is so great as to shock the conscience of the court….It also entails a consideration of the extent and enormity of the wrong, the intent of the party committing the wrong, all the circumstances, and the financial and social condition and standing of the erring party" (84 Ark. App. at 20-21; 129 S.W. 3d at 337). The second step relates to due process and "… involves an analysis of the degree of the defendant's reprehensibility or culpability; the relationship between the penalty and the harm; and the sanctions imposed in other cases for comparable misconduct" (84 Ark. App. at 21; 129 S.W. 3d at 337).

Several Arkansas Supreme court decisions in media-related and non-media-related defamation cases, dating to the late 1800s, have answered many questions about the awarding of damages. The following guidelines have been mentioned by the court:

## Damages and Moral Character/Reputation

Evidence of a plaintiff's bad moral character may be used to mitigate damages, but it may not be used as an excuse for slander (McDonald v. Louthen, 1918).

Defendants in a libel suit may mitigate damages by showing the bad reputation of a plaintiff, but a showing of bad reputation by itself does not mean that a jury can find libel *per se* and then award no damages in cases where a bad reputation means no further damage was done by the libel (Dunagan v. Upham, 1948).

A mere showing that a plaintiff has been convicted in federal court is not evidence of bad reputation (Tandy Corp. v. Bone, 1984).

## Damages and Proof Requirements

A jury cannot award punitive damages without proof of express malice (Gaines v. Belding, 1892).

Plaintiffs who prove slander *per se* are entitled to compensatory damages without having to show actual damages or special damages (Taylor v. Gumpert, 1910).

Evidence of actual damage to reputation is required for anything more than nominal damages (Armitage v. Morris, 1949).

Compensatory damages in defamation cases need not be based on proof of financial loss (Lile v. Matthews, 1980).

"Our general rule is that damages may not be allowed 'where they are speculative, resting only upon conjectural evidence or the opinions of the parties or witnesses'" (Wasp Oil, Inc. v. Arkansas Oil & Gas, Inc., 1983).

To recover damages in a defamation case, any plaintiff must prove injury to reputation (abolished presumed damages in all cases) (United Insurance Co. of America v. Murphy, 1998).

To support an award of punitive damages in a non-media slander case involving a private figure, there must be ill will, malice, or bad intent on the part of the defendant toward the plaintiff (Flynn v. McIlroy Bank & Trust Company, 1985).

### Miscellaneous Holdings

In a defamation case, mental anguish and embarrassment are proper elements of damages (Braman v. Walthall, 1949).

In multi-party suits involving compensatory damages, plaintiffs waive the right to punitive damages (Dunaway v. Troutt, 1960).

## Emotional Distress

A relatively new development concerning damages in defamation suits is the Arkansas Supreme Court's recognition of intentional infliction of emotional distress as an independent tort (M.B.M. v. Counce, 1980). This means that plaintiffs now may win separate suits charging defendants with causing emotional harm, if plaintiffs can show 1) the actor intended to inflict emotional distress or knew or should have known that emotional distress was the likely result of his conduct; 2) the conduct was extreme and outrageous, was beyond all possible bounds of decency, and was utterly intolerable in a civilized community; 3) the actions of the defendant were the cause of the plaintiff's distress; and 4) the emotional distress sustained by the plaintiff was so severe that no reasonable person could be expected to endure it (Deitsch v. Tillery, 1992).

Currently, however, the Arkansas Supreme Court has not recognized negligent infliction of emotional distress (Dalrymple v. Fields, 1982). Additionally, if a plaintiff claims only defamation and emotional distress in the same suit, a showing of damage to reputation is necessary before damages for mental suffering may be awarded (Little Rock Newspapers, Inc. v. Dodrill, 1983).

## Defenses

It has been noted above that truth is an absolute defense in defamation suits, that the media have a qualified privilege to report false and defamatory material from governmental sources (as long as the reports are an accurate representation of what was communicated and as long as information is not reported out of context), and that to win defamation suits against the media, public figures and public officials must prove actual malice (this is known as the First Amendment defense or the constitutional defense).

In 1992, the Eighth Circuit noted an extension of the qualified privilege defense (Richmond v. Southwire Co.). This case arose after a company terminated some employees and released to two local papers a statement about the situation. The statement mentioned possession, sale, and use of controlled substances, but the headline created by the newspaper implied that drug abuse was involved. The plaintiffs sued their former company rather than the newspaper.

In upholding summary judgment for defendants on defamation and false light privacy invasion charges, the court said under Arkansas law, qualified privilege exists to publish defamatory statements in good faith, to protect one's own interest, provided the publication is reasonably necessary and the privilege is not abused. In other states, this is known as the "self defense" defense. The court also noted that excessively broad publication would constitute such abuse.

Fair comment and criticism, generally reserved for statements of opinion concerning public behavior or individuals involved in issues of public interest, is another defense against defamation charges, although it has not been used frequently in Arkansas defamation cases. This defense requires that opinions be supported by providing material upon which the opinions are based, and that the opinions are not contradicted by fact.

One instance in which fair comment and criticism was successfully used involved a non-media suit brought by a University of Arkansas for Medical Sciences employee who sued UAMS in federal court because she felt her employment evaluations were libelous (Assad-Faltas v. University of Arkansas for Medical Sciences, 1989). The presiding judge concluded that common law fair comment privilege protects opinions regarding personal competence or personal characteristics related to job performance. The Eighth Circuit affirmed this decision.

Other defenses against defamation charges include consent (generally it must be direct, given by a competent adult, and witnessed); statutes of limitation (one year for criminal slander or libel, one year for civil slander, and three years for civil libel); the "single publication rule" (this permits only one libel action to be based on a defamatory article or broadcast); and retraction (this serves as a mitigating factor in damage awards).

Additionally, if publication or identification cannot be proven, the defamation suit cannot be won. The same is true if negligence cannot be shown in cases involving private individuals who sue the media.

Although some states have adopted a "neutral reportage" defense, in which the media may argue that they are mere conduits for information and thus not liable for defamatory content, Arkansas has not recognized such a defense.

# References

## Publications

Lancaster, B. (1996, June 28). Four years later, an apology. *Arkansas Times*, p. 40.

## Cases

Armitage v. Morris, 215 Ark. 383, 221 S.W.2d 9 (1949).

Assad-Faltas v. University of Arkansas for Medical Sciences, 708 F. Supp. 1026 (1989), *aff'd*, 902 F.2d 1572 (1990), *cert. denied*, 498 U.S. 905 (1990).

Baker v. State, 199 Ark. 1005, 137 S.W.2d 938 (1940).

Bland v. Verser, 299 Ark. 490, 774 S.W.2d 124 (1989).

Bloodworth v. Times Publishing Co., 128 Ark. 265, 193 S.W. 527 (1917).

Bohlinger v. Germania Life Insurance Co., 100 Ark. 477, 140 S.W. 257 (1911).

Braman v. Walthall, 215 Ark. 582, 225 S.W.2d 342 (1949).

Brandon v. Gazette Publishing Company, 234 Ark. 332, 352 S.W.2d 92 (1961).

Comes v. Cruce, 85 Ark. 79, 107 S.W. 185 (1908).

Dalrymple v. Fields, 276 Ark. 185, 633 S.W.2d 362 (1982).

Deitsch v. Tillery, 309 Ark. 401, 833 S.W.2d 760 (1992).

Dodrill v. *Arkansas Democrat*, 265 Ark. 628, 590 S.W.2d 840 (1979), *cert. denied*, 444 U.S. 1076 (1980).

Drew v. KATV Television, Inc., 293 Ark. 555, 739 S.W.2d 680 (1987).

Dun & Bradstreet, Inc. v. Nicklaus, 340 F.2d 882 (8th Cir. 1965).

Dun & Bradstreet, Inc. v. Robinson, 233 Ark. 168, 345 S.W.2d 34 (1961).

Dunagan v. Upham, 214 Ark. 66, 214 S.W.2d 786 (1948).

Dunaway v. Troutt, 232 Ark. 615, 339 S.W.2d 613 (1960).

Farris v. Tvedten, 274 Ark. 185, 623 S.W.2d 205 (1981).

Flynn v. McIlroy Bank & Trust Company, 287 Ark. 190, 697 S.W.2d 114 (1985).

Fuller v. Russell, 311 Ark. 108, 842 S.W.2d 12 (1992).

Gaines v. Belding, 56 Ark. 94, 19 S.W. 236 (1892).

Gallman v. Carnes, 254 Ark. 987, 497 S.W.2d 47 (1973).

Goodman v. Phillips, 218 Ark. 169, 235 S.W.2d 537 (1951).

Hollowell v. *Arkansas Democrat* Newspaper, 293 Ark. 329, 737 S.W.2d 646 (1987).

Honea v. King, 154 Ark. 462, 243 S.W. 74 (1922).

Janklow v. Newsweek, Inc., 788 F.2d 1300 (8th Cir. 1986).

Johnson v. Arden, No. 09-2601, slip op. (8th Cir. 2010).

Jones v. Commercial Printing Co., 249 Ark. 952, 463 S.W.2d 92 (1971).

KARK-TV v. Simon, 280 Ark. 228, 656 S.W.2d 702 (1983).

Lancaster v. The Daily Banner-News Publishing Co., Inc., 274 Ark. 145, 622 S.W.2d 671 (1981).

Lemmer v. Arkansas Gazette Company, 620 F.Supp. 1332 (E.D. Ark. 1985).

Lile v. Matthews, 268 Ark. 980, 598 S.W.2d 755 (1980).

Little Rock Newspapers, Inc. v. Dodrill, 281 Ark. 25, 660 S.W.2d 933 (1983).

Little Rock Newspapers, Inc. v. Fitzhugh, 330 Ark. 561, 954 S.W.2d 914 (1997), *cert. denied*, 523 U.S. 1095 (1998).

Luster v. Retail Credit Company, 575 F.2d 609 (8th Cir. 1978).

M.B.M. v. Counce, 268 Ark. 269, 596 S.W.2d 681 (1980).

McDonald v. Louthen, 136 Ark. 368, 206 S.W. 674 (1918).

Miller v. J.D.G. Television, Inc., No. 91-5048 (W.D. Ark. 1991).

Miller v. State, 81 Ark. 359, 99 S.W. 533 (1907).

Mitchell v. Globe International Publishing Inc., 773 F. Supp. 1235 (W.D. Ark. 1991), *sub.nom.*, Peoples Bank & Trust Co. v. Globe International, Inc., 786 F. Supp. 791 (W.D. Ark. 1992), *affirmed and remanded*, 978 F.2d 1065 (8th Cir. 1992), *on remand*, 817 F. Supp. 72 (W.D. Ark. 1993), *cert. denied*, 510 U.S. 931 (1993).

Murray v. Galbraith, 86 Ark. 50, 109 S.W. 1011 (1908).

Navorro-Monzo v. Hughes, 297 Ark. 444, 763 S.W.2d 635 (1989).

New York Times Co. v. Sullivan, 376 U.S. 254 (1964).

Northport Health Services, Inc. v. Owens, 82 Ark. App. 355, 107 S.W.3d 889 (2003)

Obaugh v. Finn, 4 Ark. 110, 37 A.D. 773 (1842).

Patton v. Cruce, 72 Ark. 421, 81 S.W. 380 (1904).

Pigg v. Ashley County Newspaper, Inc., 253 Ark. 736, 489 S.W.2d 17 (1973).

Pritchard v. Times Southwest Broadcasting, Inc., 277 Ark. 458, 642 S.W.2d 877 (1982).

Reese v. Haywood, 235 Ark. 442, 360 S.W.2d 488 (1962).

Richmond v. Southwire Co., 980 F.2d 518 (8th Cir. 1992).

Roberts v. Love, 231 Ark. 886, 333 S.W.2d 897 (1960).

Saxton v. Arkansas Gazette Co., 264 Ark. 133, 569 S.W.2d 115 (1978).

Simonson v. Lovewell, 118 Ark. 81, 175 S.W. 1036 (1912).

Sinclair Refining Co. v. Fuller, 190 Ark. 426, 79 S.W.2d 736 (1935).

Skaggs v. Johnson, 105 Ark. 254, 150 S.W. 1036 (1912).

State Press Co. v. Willett, 219 Ark. 850, 245 S.W.2d 403 (1952).

Superior Federal Bank v. Mackey, 84 Ark. App. 1, 129 S.W.3d 324 (2003).

Tandy Corp. v. Bone, 283 Ark. 399, 678 S.W.2d 312 (1984).

Taylor v. Gumpert, 96 Ark. 354, 131 S.W. 968 (1910).

Thiel v. Dove, 229 Ark. 601, 317 S.W.2d 121 (1958).

Thomson Newspaper Publishing, Inc. v. Coody, 320 Ark. 455, 896 S.W.2d 897, *cert. denied*, Coody v. Thomson Newspaper Publishing, Inc., 516 U.S. 1008 (1995).

United Insurance Co. of America v. Murphy, 331 Ark. 364, 961 S.W.2d 752 (1998).

Wal-Mart Stores, Inc. v. Lee, 348 Ark. 707, 74 S.W.3d 634 (2002).

Wasp Oil, Inc. v. Arkansas Oil & Gas, Inc., 280 Ark. 420, 658 S.W.2d 397 (1983).

Waymire v. DeHaven, 313 Ark. 687, 858 S.W.2d 69 (1993).

*West Memphis News* v. Bond, 212 Ark. 514, 206 S.W.2d 449 (1947).

Weston v. State, 258 Ark. 707, 528 S.W.2d 412 (1975).

Westridge v. Byrd, 37 Ark. App. 72, 823 S.W.2d 930 (1992).

Whiteside v. Russellville Newspapers, Inc., 2009 Ark. 135, 37 *Media Law Reporter* 1449.

Wirges v. Brewer, 239 Ark. 317, 389 S.W.2d 226 (1965).

Wortham v. Little Rock Newspapers, Inc., 273 Ark. 179, 618 S.W.2d 156 (1981).

## Statutes

Actions with Limitation of One Year, A.C.A. 16-56-104 (1987).

Actions with Limitation of Three Years, A.C.A. 16-56-105 (1987).

Communications Decency Act, 47 U.S.C. §230 (2006).

Defamatory Political Broadcasts, A.C.A. 7-6-104 (1987).

Libel and Slander, A.C.A. 16-63-207 (1987).

Penalty (Slander), A.C.A. 5-15-101 *et seq.* (1987).

Survival of Actions—Wrongs to Persons or Properties, A.C.A. 16-62-101 (1987).

Chapter 4

# Privacy

Although Cooley (1879) wrote, "The right to one's person may be said to be a right of complete immunity: the right to be let alone" (p. 29), credit for creating a national agenda concerning privacy law is generally given to Warren and Brandeis (1890) because they published the first legal treatise arguing for a right to privacy. Prosser (1960) traced the history of privacy cases occurring after publication of the Warren and Brandeis article, and he discovered a pattern.

In fact, Prosser discovered four patterns, which he described as the four torts of privacy. They were 1) intrusion upon the plaintiff's seclusion or solitude, or into his private affairs; 2) public disclosure of embarrassing private facts about the plaintiff; 3) publicity which places the plaintiff in a false light in the public eye; and 4) appropriation, for the defendant's advantage, of the plaintiff's name or likeness. In his seminal article on the four torts of privacy, Prosser noted that the right to privacy had been recognized in 30 states and the District of Columbia, either by court decision or by statute, and that in all probability it would be recognized in seven other states. He also noted that four states had rejected the right to privacy. Evidently, at the time his article was published, nine states had not yet dealt with the issue.

In 1965, Prosser's classification of privacy torts was adopted as Chapter 28A in the *Restatement of the Law (Second) of Torts 2d*, a publication of law as adopted and promulgated by the American Law Institute. In great detail, the 1977 edition of this treatise introduced "invasion of privacy" (Sec. 652A), and defined and illustrated "intrusion upon seclusion" (Sec. 652B), "appropriation of name of likeness" (Sec. 652C), "publicity given to private life" (Sec. 652D), and "publicity placing person in false light" (Sec. 652E).

Today, every state guarantees some form of privacy protection in its constitution, as part of its state code, and/or through its court decisions. Sometimes the guarantee is part of the civil code, sometimes it is incorporated into the criminal code, and sometimes it takes the form of preventing harassment or interception of communications, rather than overtly using the term privacy.

Aspects of Arkansas privacy law were first discussed in a scholarly publication by Prewett (1951), who briefly described the first "peeping Tom" law in Arkansas, passed that year as Act 62. Shortly thereafter, Evans (1952) presented an overall view of privacy law nationwide and discussed various paths Arkansas could take to recognize privacy as a tort. In 1955, after the Arkansas General Assembly clarified the "peeping Tom" law by passing Act 156 (which was expressly named "The Peeping Tom Law"), Wright noted that the law was subtitled "To Prohibit Eavesdropping, Spying and Invasions of Privacy."

In 1976, Terry outlined the concept of privacy invasion through polygraph tests by employers, noting that Arkansas polygraph licensing statutes ignored the privacy of the potential victims of the polygraph examination (p. 47). In 1979, Cochran reviewed the Arkansas rape-shield statute, which had privacy implications.

Ten years later, Wewers (1989) analyzed a freedom of information case with privacy implications. It involved actress Mercedes McCambridge, who did not want the City of Little Rock to release documents seized at the scene of a multiple murder and suicide involving her son. McCambridge claimed disclosure would be an invasion of her privacy, but the Arkansas Supreme Court ruled that public interest in the information outweighed her privacy needs (McCambridge v. City of Little Rock, 1989).

## Tort Descriptions

### Intrusion

Generally speaking, intrusion refers to physical behaviors that that invade someone's personal space or property, although the definition has been extended to include activities such as harassing telephone calls, illegal taping of telephone conversations, and hidden use of audio or video recording devices in places where an individual has a reasonable expectation of privacy. Intrusion may occur as a result of close surveillance, use of extraordinary means to gain physical or visual access to places, or trespass on private property without regard to common custom and usage. No publication is necessary for an intrusion claim to be valid, as it is the intrusive act itself that triggers the tort.

The most common defenses against charges of intrusion are consent, common custom and usage, public interest, and newsworthiness. Consent may be implied, as when a person voluntarily invites a reporter into a private home or voluntarily answers a reporter's questions, but consent is strongest when it is signed and witnessed. Also, consent is valid only if given by a person of legal age, a person who is mentally competent, and a person who has legal control over the premises involved. It should be noted that consent generally is specific to one set of circumstances and that it is revocable.

Common custom and usage refers to what is traditionally allowed or expected in a given community. For example, if it is traditional for reporters to follow police or firefighters into crime scenes or dangerous areas, either by official invitation or past experience, then the success of intrusion charges is greatly diminished. If reporters do enter private property, for the common custom and usage defense to be viable, the entry should be peaceable, and if they are asked to leave by someone who controls the property, they should leave.

The public interest defense concerns information gathering regarding public officials or governmental activities, and the information should be of the type the public needs to know, rather than of the type the public likes to know. For example, if politicians secretly hold a series of private meetings with members of organized crime, reporters who use high-power microphones to record conversations during such meetings would have a better chance with the public interest defense than they would have if the recordings had been of the politicians and their personal friends on private property.

Newsworthiness is the weakest defense for this tort, for courts have recognized many limitations to the newsgathering process on private property. It may, however, be a successful defense when the intrusive action has taken place in a public place wherein the plaintiff had no reasonable expectation of privacy or when the reporter remained on public property.

## Private, Embarrassing Facts

Publication of embarrassing private facts refers to the widespread distribution of truthful but sensitive information that someone has attempted to keep from the public. A reasonable person would find such distribution highly offensive. Such information might concern embarrassing information about a person's distant past, a loathsome disease, sexual orientation, or personal academic grades.

The common defenses related to this tort include consent, public record, minimal distribution, lack of effort on the plaintiff's part to keep the information secret, public interest, and newsworthiness. Truth is not a defense against charges linked to this tort because it is a given that the information distributed is indeed truthful, which often creates the problem in the first place.

The parameters of consent are the same as those described above. The public record defense is used when the information published is information already available to the public through some form of unsealed governmental documents (court records, arrest records, etc.), and thus is not private (see Cox Broadcasting Corp. v. Cohn, 1975).

Minimal distribution means that the information was not distributed widely. Although there is no specific number that designates a cut-off for minimal distribution, for private embarrassing facts cases, publication means either published in the mass media or distributed to a large enough sample of people such that it soon will become public knowledge.

Lack of effort on the plaintiff's part to keep the information secret means that the plaintiff did not take sufficient caution to hide the information. Although no reported Arkansas case has been decided on this defense, it was used in a 1984 California case in which publication of a person's sexual orientation was the basis for a privacy suit (Sipple v. Chronicle Publishing Co., 1984). In that case, Oliver Sipple, who had become a hero because he foiled an assassination attempt against President Ford, sued because the *San Francisco Chronicle* mentioned his homosexuality in one of its stories covering the event. Sipple lost the case because he had been a highly visible, active member of San Francisco's gay community.

The defenses of public interest and newsworthiness are the same as those defined above, although for this tort, the lines between them are far fuzzier than they are for the intrusion tort. In fact, some cases for which public interest has been used as a defense have not involved public officials, thus merging the definition of what the public needs to know with the definition of what the public likes to know.

## False Light

False light invasion of privacy refers to publication of information that mischaracterizes a person either in a bad way or in a good way, and which a reasonable person would find offensive. It may occur when photos and their captions are mixed up, when file photos are used out of context, when stories contain exaggerations or fictionalization, when quotes are misattributed or fabricated, or when voiceovers or file footage misleads the public. Generally, suits claiming false light privacy invasion involve questions of reputation, although unlike similar defamation cases, false light plaintiffs have only to prove publication of false information that embarrassed or humiliated them. Harm to reputation does not have to be proven, but cases of this nature also may include claims of emotional distress.

Defenses in false light privacy cases include truth, which is an absolute defense, consent, as defined above, and no actual malice. As for the latter defense, all jurisdictions require a finding of actual malice in false light cases involving matters of public concern, which has been the case in all reported Arkansas cases of this nature. Some jurisdictions, however, require only a finding of negligence in private-person cases not involving matters of public concern. Currently, it is unclear what fault standard courts in Arkansas will require in cases of this nature.

## Appropriation

The appropriation tort, which was the first privacy tort recognized by statute and by courts of law in the early 1900s, refers to the unauthorized use of a person's name or likeness (pictures, drawings) for commercial gain. This may occur when the name or photograph of a celebrity or other highly visible person is used to sell or promote products or fund-raising events without first gaining permission to do so. It has been extended to include look-a-likes and "sound-a-likes" of famous people, as well as false endorsements of products. Simply put, appropriation is trading on some aspect of someone else's persona to make money without that person's permission.

As with the other privacy torts, consent is a valid defense. In addition, there are exceptions for news and informational uses, incidental use, and advertising and trade purposes. News and informational uses include use in the context of providing the public with editorial content not meant to encourage purchase of any product other than the one containing the use. It is not a commercial endorsement by the person whose name or likeness is used in this way.

Incidental use involves such things as using scenes of public sidewalks and streets as passing scenery, although identifiable individuals may appear in the scenes. It also may include using a media sample, such as a book cover, to sell copies of a book, even though a model paid to be photographed for the cover is not re-paid for the additional use.

## Right to Publicity

While the appropriation tort involves money-making by people other than the plaintiff, an offshoot of appropriation, the right to publicity, involves control of one's fame and, at times, interference with one's economic ability to make money. Where control is involved, a plaintiff may want to prevent use of his or her fame to support something as benign as a positive nonprofit cause. Where a profit motive is involved, a defendant's actions may deny a plaintiff the ability to capitalize fully on his or her fame. In either case, right to publicity differs slightly from appropriation.

Consent and newsworthiness are the two most noteworthy defenses in right to publicity cases, but newsworthiness alone may not be sufficient to save a newsperson who has effectively diminished a person's ability to make money. The most famous right to publicity case involved just that, when a TV news crew filmed the entire act of a human cannonball, performing at a county fair (Zacchini v. Scripps-Howard Broadcasting Co., 1977). The performer sued and won, claiming that by showing his entire act, people would not come to the fair (or future venues) to see him perform.

# Cases

The first Arkansas Supreme Court case in which a privacy issue was raised was *Mabry v. Kettering* (1909). In this case, the plaintiff claimed an invasion of privacy by federal officials, who wanted to distribute to various locales throughout the United States the photographs they had made of him in custody. In these various locales, Mabry had been charged with violating federal criminal statutes, and the photographs were to be used for identification purposes.

In a *per curiam* decision, without addressing the privacy question, the court dissolved the restraining order that was preventing the officials from developing and distributing the photographs. The court did say, however, that the right of privacy would be an interesting question in later deliberations. On a rehearing of the case later in the year, the court affirmed its earlier decision, noting that the complaint had failed to point out any improper use of the photos which by that time had been distributed.

## Intrusion

The first Arkansas intrusion case, *Holman v. Central Arkansas Broadcasting Co.* (1979), was decided by a federal court and involved an intrusion claim by a boisterous occupant of a cell at the Russellville, Ark., police station. After his arrest, Marvin Holman, who had formerly served as a municipal judge, spent time hitting and banging on his cell door, cursing, and hollering. A radio news reporter recorded Holman's loud complaints. The federal appellate court ruled that Holman had no expectation of privacy because his statements could easily be overheard, and thus they could be recorded and published.

The first intrusion decision by the Arkansas Supreme Court was handed down in 1981. *CBM of Central Arkansas v. Bemel* involved alleged harassment by a bill collector who, over a 10-month period, sent Geneva Bemel about 50 collection letters and called her approximately 70 times, often at irregular hours at her home and at her business, despite her objections. The reason for the letters and calls was that Ms. Bemel's son had shot himself in an unsuccessful suicide attempt, and his hospital bill was partially unpaid. The court affirmed a Pulaski County Circuit Court opinion that the phone calls were excessive, and that frequent phone calls to a debtor from a collection agency could be an invasion of privacy.

*Dunlap v. McCarty* (1984), the next intrusion case decided by the Arkansas Supreme Court, reversed a lower court finding of intrusion. The high court based its decision on the fact that the statute of limitations had run out. This case, like *CBM of Central Arkansas v.*

*Bemel*, involved phone calls, but there were only two such calls. The plaintiff alleged the calls were made maliciously, they invaded his privacy, and they destroyed his personal life. The court, though not ruling on the intrusion claim, noted that it could not find any successful intrusion cases based on one or two phone calls.

In the most recent Arkansas intrusion case, a nonmedia case involving the question of consent governing a search of private property by private individuals, the Arkansas Supreme Court found that when the scope of consent is not clear, intrusion may occur (Wal-Mart Stores, Inc. v. Lee, 2002).

Court judgments about actions on private property that do or do not constitute intrusion also have been litigated recently. For example, in *Hudspeth v. State* (2002), the Arkansas Supreme Court noted that people have no reasonable expectation of privacy in an open field; in *Walley v. State* (2003), the same court ruled that there is no "... objectively reasonable expectation of privacy in the area around a rental residence" (353 Ark. at 606, 112 S.W.3d at 360).

In *Russell v. State* (2004), the court said, "An expectation of privacy in driveways and walkways, which are commonly used by visitors to approach dwellings, is not generally considered reasonable" (85 Ark. App. 468 at 474; 157 S.W. 3d 561 at 566).

## Private, Embarrassing Facts

The first Arkansas embarrassing facts privacy case was not reported in the legal literature, but it was a well-publicized trial decided by a federal court jury in Little Rock (Siscoe v. Fawcett Publications, Inc., 1977). The suit was filed in 1974, after *Startling Detective* magazine ran a story of a shoot-out at the home of William and Mona Siscoe, in which their daughter was killed. The magazine also ran several photographs of the daughter, one of which showed a bleeding bullet wound in her back (Siscoes lose, 1977).

Counsel for the Siscoes said they were embarrassed and humiliated, and that the Siscoes contended the article had no news value because it was written three years after the incident. The jury, though, rejected the $500,000 privacy claim, finding unanimously that the article was a matter of public interest that did not invade the Siscoes' privacy.

In 1980, an unusual private facts case was heard by the federal court in the western district of Arkansas (Boyd v. Thompson). In this case, the parents of a deceased child sued the *Northwest Arkansas Times* for printing the name of the child, the date of his death, and the circumstances surrounding his death. The federal court ruled for the newspaper, noting that the Arkansas Supreme Court would not recognize a relational right to privacy.

A 1987 case decided by the U.S. Court of Appeals for the Eighth Circuit involved a question of private facts, but the court ruled that the conduct involved did not begin to meet the standard of extreme and outrageous conduct (Wood v. National Computer Systems, Inc.). In this case, an elementary school teacher in Fort Smith, Ark., sued a computer firm because it mistakenly sent to someone else her scores on a mandated teacher test. The court said that disclosure of private information to one other person was not publicity of a highly objectionable kind.

## False Light

The first reported Arkansas privacy decision involving a false light privacy claim occurred in 1979. In *Dodrill v. Arkansas Democrat Co.* (1979), the Arkansas Supreme Court dismissed a false light privacy claim against the Arkansas Democrat Co., after its newspaper mistakenly said Dodrill had failed the bar exam. Dodrill was a lawyer who had been suspended from practicing law and who had been required to retake the bar exam. When his name was not among those on the official list of those passing the exam, the newspaper assumed he had failed, which was not true.

The lower court had awarded Dodrill $40,000 for mental suffering, but the high court reversed, noting that the information had not been published with actual malice, which was required because the case involved a matter of public interest. The court also said that Dodrill would have had to have shown clear and convincing evidence of actual malice.

Four years later, the federal court for the western district of Arkansas ruled on two combined privacy cases involving claims of false light, intrusion, private facts, and appropriation (*Williams v. ABC*, 1983). The issue in both cases was whether or not a television network should be made to produce out-takes of footage upon which the invasion of privacy claims were being made, to help the plaintiffs prove those claims. The court agreed that the out-takes should be handed over.

The cases arose after the ABC television news program *20/20* showed a segment in which a Boone County (Ark.) surgeon was characterized as routinely performing unnecessary surgery, and in which the surgeon was shown refusing to answer questions during an ambush interview. One of the surgeon's patients also was suing because her hip surgery had been filmed without her consent and shown on the same ABC program.

It was eight years later that the Arkansas Supreme Court decided another false light claim. This one was prompted by a letter distributed to several governmental officials, a reporter, and other individuals (Dodson v. Dicker, 1991). David Dicker sued after Dodson, in his letter, accused Dicker of a variety of negative actions associated with the State Board of Therapy Technology, the president of which was Dicker's wife. The Arkansas Supreme Court reversed the lower court's award of $12,000, noting that in this matter of public concern, there was no clear and convincing evidence of actual malice toward Dicker.

The most recent false light privacy case originating in Arkansas gained national attention and was taken to the United States Supreme Court (Mitchell v. Globe International Publishing, Inc., 1991). It began when the *Sun*, a tabloid publication owned by Globe International, ran a fictitious story in 1990 about an aged Australian newspaper carrier who had become pregnant by one of the customers on her route. Pictures of Nellie Mitchell, a resident of Mountain Home, Ark., appeared on the cover of the tabloid and with the story.

Mitchell sued in federal court for false light privacy invasion and libel, and after a lengthy series of court battles, she prevailed on the privacy charge. Without comment, the U.S. Supreme Court let stand the $1 million judgment awarded her by the lower courts (Globe International Publishing, Inc. v. Peoples Bank and Trust Company, 1993). The jury had awarded Mitchell $1.5 million, but on appeal, the courts had reduced the damages for privacy invasion and emotional distress to $1 million.

## Appropriation

The only appropriation case to reach the Arkansas Supreme Court was the privacy case in which the court officially recognized the tort of invasion of privacy (Olan Mills v. Dodd, 1962). In this case, a photography studio had, without Mary Dodd's knowledge or consent, printed her picture on 150,000 advertising postcards to be mailed throughout Arkansas and the surrounding states. The court said that even though the defendant had admitted it was the result of a mistake, it was still unlawful appropriation, and therefore the lower court's award of $2,500 in damages was upheld.

## Constitutional and Statutory Provisions

Although Arkansas technically does not recognize by statute any of the traditional four torts of privacy, its constitution and many state statutes do protect against some forms of privacy invasion. In fact, the Arkansas Supreme Court in 2002 said, "In considering our constitution together with the statutes, rules, and case law mentioned above [in the case at hand], it is clear to this court that Arkansas has a rich and compelling tradition of protecting individual privacy and that a fundamental right to privacy is implicit in the Arkansas Constitution" (Jegley v. Picado, 349 Ark. at 631-32, 80 S.W.3d at 349-50). Constitutional guarantees are found in eight sections of Article 2, the Declaration of Rights (1874). Section 2, "Freedom and Independence," protects people's rights to property and reputation, as well as their right to pursue their own happiness. Section 4, "Right of Assembly and of Petition," protects people's right of association, and Section 8, "Criminal Charges—Self-incrimination—Due Process—Double Jeopardy—Bail," protects against bearing witness against oneself.

Section 13, "Redress of Wrongs," guarantees the right to remedy in the laws for all injuries or wrongs received to person, property, or character, while Section 15, "Unreasonable Searches and Seizures," makes guarantees similar to the United States Constitution's Fourth Amendment. Sections 24 and 25, "Religious Liberty" and "Protection of Religion," respectively, protect religious freedoms, and Section 29, "Enumeration of Rights of People not Exclusive of Other Rights—Protection Against Encroachment," basically guarantees citizens that a given right does not have to be included in the Constitution in order for it to be a protected right.

One or more aspects of each of these guarantees may be interpreted to include some form of a right to privacy. Similarly, taken together much in the same way that Justice Douglas found a right to privacy in the U.S. Constitution (Griswold v. Connecticut, 1965), these rights form a "shadow" from which a right to privacy flows.

Concerning statutory provisions involving privacy, the one enacted earliest (1947) by the Arkansas General Assembly protects citizens from physical harassment (A.C.A. 5-71-208), including surveillance, annoyance, and physical abuse. A subsequent section protects citizens from harassing communications (A.C.A. 5-71-209), including those by telephone, telegraph, mail, or any other form of written communication. Harassment, under this law, can take place whether or not a conversation ensues.

As noted above, a 1951 statute, later clarified by a 1955 revision, protected Arkansas citizens from "peeping Toms" and other eavesdroppers. Eventually, this statute evolved into an anti-loitering statute (A.C.A. 5-71-213), subsection (a)(8) of which prohibits people from lingering or remaining "... on or about the premises of another for the purpose of spying upon or invading the privacy of another."

In 1967, Arkansas adopted its Freedom of Information Act (A.C.A. 25-19-101 et seq.), which contains typical exemptions involving personal information. These include such items as personnel information, business information, and medical, scholastic, and adoption information.

In addition to the exemptions contained in the Freedom of Information Act, more than 50 other statutes provide exemptions or exceptions to the law. While many of these merely expand upon the above-mentioned exemptions, some include previously unlisted areas such as vital records, domestic relations cases, and judicial ethics complaints. In 1977, Arkansas adopted its rape-shield statute (A.C.A. 16-42-101), titled "Admissibility of Evidence of Victim's Prior Sexual Conduct." Essentially, the statute prohibits defendants in rape cases from introducing information about victims' sexual history.

Another statute involving communications concerns the interception and recording of wire or telephonic communications (A.C.A. 5-60-120). This statute prohibits a person from intercepting, recording, or possessing a recording of any wire or telephonic communication unless such a person is a party to the communication or unless one of the parties to the communication has given prior consent to such interception and recording.

Finally, it should be noted that in 1999, the Arkansas General Assembly created a statute making video voyeurism a crime (A.C.A.

5-16-101). The statute reads, "It is unlawful to use any camera, videotape, photo-optical, photo-electric, or any other image recording device for the purpose of secretly observing, viewing, photographing, filming, or videotaping a person present in a residence, place of business, school, or other structure, or any room or particular location within that structure, where that person is in a private area out of public view, has a reasonable expectation of privacy, and has not consented to the observation." The law, however, exempts court-ordered video monitoring or recording, private security monitoring by or at the direction of occupants of residences or the owners of structures named within the statute, and recording or monitoring by law enforcement officers acting within the official scope of their duties.

In 2007, the video voyeurism statute was amended by Act 187 to prohibit use of "... a camcorder, motion picture camera, photographic camera of any type, or other equipment that is concealed or disguised to secretly or surreptitiously videotape, film, photograph, record, or view by electronic means a person for the purpose of viewing any portion of the person's body that is covered with clothing and for which the person has a reasonable expectation of privacy ..." without the person's knowledge or consent.

While Arkansas' reported litigation in the area of privacy is limited almost entirely to questions of law described by Prosser's (1960) four torts, it is clear that to understand the broad-based ramifications of privacy law in the state, journalists cannot rely exclusively upon their knowledge of court proceedings. Indeed, lack of knowledge about both the state's constitutional roots for privacy protection and the state's statutory provisions protecting various forms of privacy would yield a very narrow understanding of privacy law in Arkansas.

# References

## Publications

Cochran, M. (1979). Act 197 of 1977: Arkansas' rape-shield statute. *Arkansas Law Review 32*(4), 806-815.

Cooley, T.M. (1879). *A Treatise on the Law of Torts or the Wrongs Which Arise Independent of Contracts* Chicago: Callaghan and Company.

Evans, J.H. (1952). The right of Privacy. *Arkansas Law Review and Bar Association Journal, 6*(4), pp. 459-472.

Prewett, B. (1951). The crimination of peeping Tom and other men of vision. *Arkansas Law Review and Bar Association Journal, 5*(4), 388-389.

Prosser, W.L. (1960). Privacy. *California Law Review, 48*(3), 388-389.

*Restatement of the Law (Second) of Torts 2d.* (1977). St. Paul, MN: The American Law Institute.

Siscoes lose privacy invasion case. (1977, April 29). *Arkansas Democrat*, p. A6.

Terry, R.M. (1976). Privacy: The polygraph in employment. *Arkansas Law Review 30*(1), 35-48.

Warren, S.D. & Brandeis, L.D. (1890). The right of privacy. Harvard *Law Review, 4*(5), 193-220.

Wewers, E. (1989-90). Constitutional law-The right of nondisclosure-The unintended victim of the Markle murders. *McCambridge v. City of Little Rock*, 298 Ark. 219, 766 S.W.2d 909 (1989). *UALR Law Journal, 12*(2), 423-439.

Wright R. R. (1955). Peeping Toms, eavesdroppers and invaders of privacy. *Arkansas Law Review and Bar Association Journal, 9*(4), 397-399.

## Cases

Boyd v. Thompson, 6 Media Law Reporter 1020 (W.D. Ark. 1980).

CBM of Central Arkansas v. Bemel, 274 Ark. 223, 623 S.W.2d 518 (1981).

Cox Broadcasting Corp. v. Cohn, 420 U.S. 469 (1975).

Dodrill v. Arkansas Democrat Co., 265 Ark. 628, 590 S.W.2d 840 (1979), *cert. denied*, 444 U.S. 1076 (1980).

Dodson v. Dicker, 306 Ark. 108, 812 S.W.2d 97 (1991).

Dunlap v. McCarty, 284 Ark. 5, 678 S.W.2d 361 (1984).

Griswold v. Connecticut, 381 U.S. 479 (1965).

Holman v. Central Arkansas Broadcasting Co., 610 F.2d 542 (8th Cir. 1979).

Hudspeth v. State, 349 Ark. 315, 78 S.W.3d 99 (2002).

Jegley v. Picado, 349 Ark. 600, 80 S.W.3d 332 (2002).

Mabry v. Kettering, 89 Ark. 551, 117 S.W. 746 (1909), *rehearing*, 92 Ark. 81, 122 S.W. 115 (1909).

McCambridge v. City of Little Rock, 298 Ark. 219, 766 S.W.2d 909 (1989).

Mitchell v. Globe International Publishing Inc., 773 F.Supp. 1235 (W.D. Ark. 1991), *sub.nom.*, Peoples Bank & Trust Co. v. Globe International, Inc., 786 F.Supp. 791 (W.D. Ark 1992), *affirmed and remanded*, 978 F.2d 1065 (8th Cir. 1992), *on remand*, 817 F.Supp. 72 (W.D. Ark. 1993), *cert. denied*, Globe International, Inc. v. Peoples Bank and Trust Co., 510 U.S. 931 (1993).

Olan Mills v. Dodd, 234 Ark. 495, 353 S.W.2d 22 (1962).

Russell v. State, 85 Ark. App. 468, 157 S.W.3d 561 (2004).

Sipple v. Chronicle Publishing Co., 154 Cal. App. 3d 1040 (1984).

Siscoe v. Fawcett Publications, Inc. Docket No. LR-74-C-242, U.S. District Court (E.D. Ark. 1977).

Walley v. State, 353 Ark. 586, 112 S.W.3d 349 (2003).

Wal-Mart Stores, Inc. v. Lee, 348 Ark. 707, 74 S.W.3d 634 (2002).

Williams v. ABC, 96 F.R.D. 658 (W.D. Ark. 1983).

Wood v. National Computer Systems, Inc. 814 F.2d 544 (8th Cir. 1987).

Zacchini v. Scripps-Howard Broadcasting Co., 433 U.S. 562 (1977).

## Constitutions and Statutes

Admissibility of Evidence of Victim's Prior Sexual Conduct, A.C.A. 16-42-101 (1987).

Arkansas Constitution, Article 2, Sections 2, 4, 8, 13, 15, 24, 25, and 29 (1874).

Arkansas Freedom of Information Act, A.C.A. 25-19-101 *et seq.* (1987).

Crime of Video Voyeurism, A.C.A. 5-16-101 (1987).

Harassment Communications, A.C.A. 5-71-209 (1987).

Harassment, A.C.A. 5-71-208 (1987).

Interception and Recording, A.C.A. 5-60-120 (1987).

Loitering, A.C.A. 5-71-213 (1987).

Chapter 5

# News-gathering Issues

In addition to the more common media-related legal issues such as defamation, invasion of privacy, freedom of information, and obscenity, a variety of lesser known aspects of law occasionally affects media practitioners. These include source protection, access to news events, harassment, obstruction of governmental operations, disorderly conduct, and taping of telephone conversations.

## Source Protection

Although the U.S. Supreme Court in *Branzburg v. Hayes* (1972) refused to recognize a reporter's First Amendment right not to disclose sources to a grand jury, guidelines provided by Justice Potter Stewart and two other dissenting justices in that case have been widely adopted by many lower courts. The guidelines indicate that before a reporter may be compelled to disclose a source to any governmental official, there must be a demonstration that all of the following are true:

(a) there is probable cause to believe that the newsman has information that is clearly relevant to a specific probable violation of law;
(b) the information sought cannot be obtained by alternative means less destructive of First Amendment rights; and
(c) there is a compelling and overriding interest in the information.

Application of these guidelines generally has depended upon the type of court involved (grand jury versus trial court), the type of case being tried (criminal versus civil), and the litigation status of the reporter (litigant versus non-litigant).

While the guidelines have been applied on an *ad hoc* basis in both federal and non-federal jurisdictions, more than half of the states have adopted individual shield laws to protect reporters from disclosing their sources. Arkansas first adopted a shield law in 1936. In 2011, the Arkansas General Assembly amended the shield law, which now reads as follows:

> "Before any editor, reporter, or other writer for any newspaper, periodical, radio station, television station, or Internet news source, or publisher of any newspaper, periodical, or Internet news source, or manager or owner of any radio station shall be required to disclose to any grand jury or to any other authority the source of information used as the basis for any article he or she may have written, published, or broadcast, it must be shown that the article was written, published, or broadcast in bad faith, with malice, and not in the interest of the public welfare." (A.C.A. 16-85-510)

With the amended language, the statute finally recognizes TV broadcast stations and Internet news sources as being covered by the shield law.

In 1983, in a Federal District Court privacy case (discussed above in Chapter 4), the judge ruled that the Arkansas shield law also applied to television journalists (Williams v. ABC), thus extending the statute's coverage to all of the primary mass media. On the other hand, he ruled that the statute applies only to sources, and therefore the video out-takes being sought in that case were not protected.

Tull (1996) noted that the *Williams* court "... recognized that journalists have a qualified privilege for unpublished materials." He also noted that in three unreported Arkansas cases, courts have supported the idea "... that reporters have a qualified privilege under the First Amendment and are not required to testify as witnesses about information obtained during the news-gathering process" (p. 2). He continued, "Therefore, absent a sufficient showing that the materials sought were relevant or that the materials could not be obtained elsewhere, any subpoena requesting the materials should be quashed."

The only other reported case involving the Arkansas shield law is *Saxton v. Arkansas Gazette Co.* (1978). In this case, a civil proceeding, the plaintiff asked the court to compel an *Arkansas Gazette* reporter to reveal a source to whom she had referred in an article she had written about a meeting of the Arkansas Soil and Water Commission. In her story, she wrote that Saxton had falsified the minutes of the meeting, and in testimony, it became clear that she had received an anonymous letter to that effect. At some point, she guessed at the identity of the anonymous letter and shared that guess with her editor and a deputy prosecuting attorney, but later it was determined that her guess was incorrect.

Several aspects of this decision are worth noting. First, the court recognized the strength of the Arkansas shield law.

Second, the court ruled that although the original shield law was passed to amend and modify the criminal law in Arkansas, "... use of the words 'to any other authority' in this section of the Act clearly indicates that the privilege asserted here is applicable to civil proceedings" (264 Ark. at 136; 569 S.W.2d at 117).

Third, despite the fact that the statute had been passed and amended well before the U.S. Supreme Court in 1964 created the definition of "actual malice" as "knowing falsehood or reckless disregard of truth" (New York Times Co. v. Sullivan), the Arkansas Supreme Court ascribed that meaning to the "bad faith, with malice, and not in the interest of the public welfare" phrasing of the Arkansas law, at least in cases involving a public official.

Watkins (1989) reported that a 1967 Arkansas circuit court decision held that the Arkansas shield law did not protect sources for unpublished articles, and that an informal attorney general's opinion confirmed that *anyone* who furnishes information is a source (even the author of a letter to the editor). Concerning the former revelation, it remains unclear as to whether the statute's reference to "written" material means that such material also must be published or broadcast to be protected.

A 1993 newspaper story about the first phase of a defamation trial in northwest Arkansas (Thomson Newspaper Publishing, Inc. v. Coody) reported that one of the defendants was ordered by the Arkansas circuit court judge hearing the case to reveal the names of people whose information contributed to an editorial and article published by the defendant's newspaper (Hursey, 1993). Relying on the Arkansas shield law, the defendant at first refused to name his sources, but eventually he did reveal them and they testified in court.

It should be noted that the Arkansas shield law pertains to all sources, not merely confidential sources. It also should be noted that giving up the name of a source after promising confidentiality may lead to a breach of contract suit by the source. The U.S. Supreme Court has recognized the validity of such action (Cohen v. Cowles Media Co., 1991).

## Newsroom Searches

With passage of the Privacy Protection Act of 1980 (42 U.S.C.A. 2000aa), Congress limited federal, state, and local law enforcement agencies from obtaining warrants to search for or seize any work product materials possessed by a person reasonably believed to have a purpose to disseminate to the public a newspaper, book, broadcast, or other similar form of public communication. This means that generally speaking, items such as reporters' notes, tapes, drafts of stories, and photographs would be protected against seizure through search warrants.

Law enforcement officials can, however, obtain search warrants for a reporter's materials if they believe the following: that the reporter is engaged in criminal activity to which the materials relate; that seizure is necessary to prevent a death or serious bodily injury; that the reporter would destroy or conceal the materials if served with a subpoena; or that the reporter has not handed over the materials in response to a court order, and further delay would obstruct justice.

## Access to News Events

In Arkansas, news reporters have special, limited privileges to cover news events from which the general public may be excluded. For example, the Arkansas Code Annotated contains the following section: "A person commits the offense of failure to disperse if, during a riot or an unlawful assembly, he refuses or knowingly fails to disperse when ordered to do so by a law enforcement officer or other person engaged in enforcing or executing the law" (A.C.A. 5-71-206). The section, however, continues, "It is a defense to a prosecution under this section that the actor was a news reporter or other person observing or recording the events on behalf of the news media not knowingly obstructing efforts by a law enforcement officer or other person engaged in enforcing or executing the law to control or abate the riot or unlawful assembly."

## Trespass

The Arkansas criminal trespass statute states that trespassing occurs when people purposely enter or remain "unlawfully in or upon a vehicle or the premises of another person" (A.C.A. 5-39-203). Reporters (and the general public) maintain a right to enter property that is sometimes open to the public, such as places of business or unfenced, unposted land, but if the owner or anyone else with authority to do so orders a reporter off of the property, the reporter must leave.

The statute governing access to places of business reads, "Any person who enters a public place of business in this state, or upon the premises thereof, and is requested or ordered to leave therefrom by the owner, manager, or any employee and, after having been so requested or ordered to leave, refuses so to do, shall be guilty of a trespass ..." (A.C.A. 4-70-101). In *Culhane v. State* (1984), the Arkansas Supreme Court upheld this statute, ruling that it was not overly broad.

## Harassment and Loitering

Harassment charges might be another problem faced by journalists conducting investigative research. Among other behaviors, harassment can occur when a person, without good cause, (1) follows another person in or about a public place; (2) engages in conduct or repeatedly commits acts that alarm or seriously annoy another person and that serve no legitimate purpose; or (3) places a person under surveillance by remaining present outside his or her school, place of employment, vehicle, other place occupied by the person, or residence, other than the residence of the defendant, for no purpose other than to harass, alarm, or annoy (A.C.A. 5-71-208). While people such as law enforcement officers, private investigators, attorneys, process servers, bail bondsmen, and store detectives are exempt from this statute if they are acting within the reasonable scope of their duties, reporters are not exempt.

Additionally, as noted in Chapter 4, Arkansas has an anti-loitering statute that prohibits people from lingering or remaining "on or about the premises of another for the purpose of spying upon or invading the privacy of another" (A.C.A. 5-71-213).

## Obstructing Governmental Operations

Akin to harassment is obstructing governmental operations. Section 5-54-102 of the Arkansas Code Annotated states that it is illegal for a person to knowingly obstruct, impair, or hinder the performance of any governmental function. This is a fairly broad phrase, and it could include behaviors that interfere with law enforcement, behaviors that disrupt public meetings, or behaviors that interrupt workers in governmental offices.

## Disorderly Conduct

Obstruction of governmental operations also may occur through disorderly conduct, defined by statute as follows:

> A person commits the offense of disorderly conduct if, with the purpose to cause public inconvenience, annoyance, or alarm or recklessly creating a risk thereof, he:
> ...
> (2) makes unreasonable or excessive noise; or
> (3) in a public place, uses abusive or obscene language, or makes an obscene gesture, in a manner likely to provoke a violent or disorderly response; or
> (4) disrupts or disturbs any lawful assembly or meeting of persons; or
> (5) obstructs vehicular or pedestrian traffic (A.C.A. 5-71-207).

Clearly, journalists may be tempted to exhibit such disorderly behaviors during public meetings from which they are being unwillingly ejected, or during disagreements with law enforcement officers about access to crime, accident, or disaster scenes, but such behaviors also could occur during vigorous interviews with unwilling sources or during a variety of reportorial activities that are not going well for the reporter. It would be good advice in such situations to remain calm and to refrain from making gestures that would provoke disorderly responses.

## Telephone Conversations and Stored Communications

It is not illegal in Arkansas to tape your own telephone conversations without telling the other party or parties with whom you are speaking (A.C.A. 5-60-120). On July 1, 1979, however, Southwestern Bell Telephone Company began requiring that callers obtain written permission to record others involved in telephone conversations with them or that callers provide some form of "recorder tone" at approximately 15-second intervals (Southwestern Bell Telephone Co., 1979). If this procedure is not followed and there are complaints about recording of telephone conversations, Southwestern Bell may terminate telephone service to those engaged in unannounced recording.

In addition, the Federal Communications Commission requires broadcasters to notify all parties to a call that is being recorded for broadcast purposes (47 C.F.R. 73.1206). Federal law also makes it illegal to intercept electronic communications (Electronic Communications Privacy Act; 18 U.S.C. §2510 *et seq.*) or to intentionally access, without authorization, any remote computer service or electronic communication service and "alter" or "obtain" any communication while in storage (Stored Communications Act; 18 U.S.C. §2701 *et seq.*). The Act criminalizes unauthorized access to stored remote computer files.

In February 2010, student plaintiffs filed a class action lawsuit alleging that the Lower Merion School District in Pennsylvania violated their privacy and violated the Stored Communications Act by activating and accessing school issued laptops students used while at home. The accessed files included screen shots of students while in their bedrooms. In October 2010, in an unreported decision by the federal district court in Eastern Pennsylvania, the school district agreed to pay a judgment of $610,000 (Robbins v. Lower Merion School District).

Because all federal statutes are applicable to every state, it is important to note that Arkansas colleges and school districts that issue computers to students for use at home are subject to the Stored Communications Act.

## Video Voyeurism

As noted above in the chapter on privacy, the Arkansas General Assembly recently made video voyeurism a crime (A.C.A. 5-16-101). In essence, the statute forbids secret observation and image recording of people who have a reasonable expectation of privacy in private areas that are out of the public view. The law exempts security monitoring by or at the direction of occupants of residences, security monitoring by owners or administrators of structures named within the statute, and video monitoring by law enforcement officers acting within the official scope of their duties. This statute was extended in 2007 to include virtually any secret, visual recording of a person's body parts that are covered by clothing, for the purpose of viewing those body parts without the person's knowledge or consent.

It should be noted the 2007 amendment essentially divides the offense of video voyeurism into two classes, the first, a felony, by secretly video recording in a private place where one has a reasonable expectation of privacy (whether one is clothed or not), and the second, a misdemeanor, by secretly video recording in any place body parts that are covered by clothing.

# References


## Publications

Hursey, L. (1993, Dec. 3). Court rules against ex-publisher. *Northwest Arkansas Times*, p. 1.

Tull, J.E. III. (1996, July 18). High standards required for obtaining unpublished photographs. *Arkansas Press Association Member Bulletin*, p. 2.

Watkins, J. J. (1989) Confidential sources. *Arkansas Media Law Handbook.* Little Rock: Arkansas Bar Association.

## Cases

Branzburg v. Hayes, 408 U.S. 665 (1972).

Cohen v. Cowles Media Co., 501 U.S. 663 (1991).

Culhane v. State, 282 Ark. 286, 668 S.W.2d 24 (1984).

New York Times Co. v. Sullivan, 376 U.S. 254 (1964).

Robbins v. Lower Merion School District, CV 10-665 (E. D. Pennsylvania, August 30, 2010).

Saxton v. Arkansas Gazette Co., 264 Ark. 133, 569 S.W.2d 115 (1978).

Thomson Newspaper Publishing, Inc. v. Coody, 320 Ark. 455, 896 S.W.2d 897, *cert. denied*, Coody v. Thomson Newspaper Publishing, Inc., 516 U.S. 1008 (1995).

Williams v. ABC, 96 F.R.D. 658 (W.D. Ark. 1983).

## Statutes

Broadcast of Telephone Conversations, 47 C.F.R. 73.1206 (1988).

Crime of Video Voyeurism, A.C.A. 5-16-101 (1987).

Criminal Trespass, A.C.A. 5-39-203 (1987).

Disclosure of Newspaper, Periodical, or Radio Station Sources, A.C.A. 16-85-510 (1987).

Disorderly Conduct, A.C.A. 5-71-207 (1987).

Failure to Disperse, A.C.A. 5-71-206 (1987).

Harassment, A.C.A. 5-71-208 (1987).

Interception and Recording, A.C.A. 5-60-120 (1987).

Loitering, A.C.A. 5-71-213 (1987).

Obstructing Governmental Operations, A.C.A. 5-54-102 (1987).

Privacy Protection Act of 1980, 42 U.S.C. §2000aa (2006).

Right to Select Customers—Penalty for Customer's Failure to Comply, A.C.A. 4-70-101 (1987).

Stored Communications Act, 18 U.S.C. §2701 *et seq.* (2006).

Wire Interception and Interception of Oral Communications, 18 U.S.C. §2510 *et seq.* (2006).

## Other Private Regulations

Recording of Two-way Telephone Conversations, Southwestern Bell Telephone Co. General Exchange Tariff 6.1.1.D. (1979).

Chapter 6

# Freedom of Information

In 1967, the Arkansas General Assembly passed Act 93, to be known as the Freedom of Information Act of 1967 (A.C.A. 25-19-101 *et seq.*). The intent section of the act stated, "It is vital in a democratic society that public business be performed in an open and public manner so that the electors shall be advised of the performance of public officials and of the decisions that are reached in public activity and in making public policy" (A.C.A. 25-19-102). It is noteworthy that the Arkansas FOIA should be regarded as a people's law, rather than as a special statute for members of the media.

Unlike some other states that have separate statutes to open governmental records and governmental meetings to the public, the Arkansas law incorporates guarantees for both. Individuals who negligently violate any provisions of the statute "... shall be punished by a fine of not more than two hundred dollars ($200) or thirty (30) days in jail, or both, or a sentence of appropriate public service or education, or both" (A.C.A. 25-19-104).

To clarify the use of electronic signatures and electronic transactions within the State of Arkansas, the Arkansas General Assembly in 2001 passed the Uniform Electronic Transactions Act (A.C.A. 25-32-101 *et seq.*). Section 117 of this law describes creation and retention of electronic records and conversion of written records by governmental agencies, leaving it up to each governmental agency to "... determine whether, and to the extent which, it will create and retain electronic records and convert written records to electronic records."

Act 569, passed by the Arkansas General Assembly in 2009, amends a section of the Local Government Title (A.C.A. 14-14-111 – electronic records) and requires that county officials who maintain public records in electronic form retain administrative rights to the data and complete access to all records, and that contracts with electronic records providers include provisions to that effect.

## Public Records

Public records are defined under the law as "... writings, recorded sounds, films, tapes, or data compilations in any form, required by law to be kept or otherwise kept, and which constitute a record of the performance or lack of performance of official functions which are or should be carried out by a public official or employee, a governmental agency, or any other agency wholly or partially supported by public funds or expending public funds. All records maintained in public offices or by public employees within the scope of their employment shall be presumed to be public records" (A.C.A. 25-19-103). Occasionally, changes are made in the Arkansas FOIA, either to include or exclude certain records. In 2011, through Act 210, the 88th Arkansas General Assembly added "improvement districts" to the entities covered by the Arkansas FOIA.

In 2001, the Arkansas General Assembly amended the Arkansas Freedom of Information Act to specifically include electronic records and computer-based information. Under the new definition of public records, however, a section was added to clarify that the term "public records" does not mean software acquired by purchase, lease, or license.

In 2007, the Arkansas Supreme Court adopted Administrative Order 19, which granted public access to "... all court records, regardless of the manner of creation, method of collection, form of storage, or the form in which the records are maintained" (*In re* Adoption of Administrative Order Number 19 – Access to Court Records). Of course, the court recognized exceptions to access, including such information as that which already is excluded from access pursuant to federal law, state law, or court order; information concerning Social Security numbers and certain financial account numbers; information expunged or sealed by courts; notes, communications, and deliberative materials regarding decisions of judges, jurors, court staff, and judicial agencies; and litigant addresses and phone numbers.

The description of the exclusion for "litigant addresses" was modified in 2008 to read as follows: "All home and business addresses of petitioners who request anonymity when seeking a domestic order of protection" (A.C.A. 9-15-203 (Repl. 2008)). The explanation for this change was that keeping all litigants' addresses confidential was too broad and unworkable, especially concerning their necessity regarding summonses and judgments.

Administrative Order No. 19 provides that a "court record" does not include information maintained in the record by other agencies or entities and which are not a "necessary" part of the litigation or proceeding. That limitation would presume to include records maintained by other agencies shared in the same database within a court record. The order notes, however, "If the information is disclosed in open court and is part of a verbatim transcript of court proceedings or included in trial transcript source materials, the information is not excluded from public access."

Administrative Order No. 19 further provides for a procedure to obtain information sealed by this order or by court order. A person requesting such information bears the burden of showing that reasonable circumstances require a deviation from the order, that public interest in disclosure outweighs the harm in disclosure, or that the information sought does not fall within the exceptions requiring it to be sealed under the order.

In keeping with its policy to make court records electronically accessible, Administrative Order No. 19, in Section V, established a provision for Internet access to court records. While the program is not fully developed (only six counties were fully online in 2011), county court records may be searched on the Arkansas Judiciary Administrative Office of the Courts Web site, *https://arkansas.gov/aoc.*

Another change in one form of public access to a specific type of court was made in 2011 by another Administrative Order, as noted in the subsequent chapter on "Media and the Courts." In this case, the Arkansas Supreme Court amended Administrative Order No. 6(c)(3) to exclude drug courts from taping and broadcasting.

The Arkansas FOIA also provides that except for certain exemptions listed in the statute or provided by laws specifically enacted to provide otherwise, "... all public records shall be open to inspection and copying by any citizen of the State of Arkansas during the regular business hours of the custodian of records (A.C.A. 25-19-105).

A new twist concerning public records is the requirement that certain records be placed on Web sites. Two such requirements were codified as Acts 1163 and 303 of the 2011 Arkansas General Assembly session. The former, known as the Arkansas Open Checkbook Act, requires the Department of Finance and Administration (DFA) to create and maintain a searchable Web site that allows the public free access to aggregate information compiled by the agency concerning state agency expenditures, including those of colleges and universities. The latter, known as the Arkansas Financial Transparency Act, requires the DFA to maintain a publicly accessible database of state agency expenditures.

As of 2011, the statute listed 20 "records" exemptions, including income tax returns, medical records, scholastic records, adoption records, grand jury minutes, undisclosed investigations by law enforcement agencies of suspected criminal activity, personnel records (to the extent that disclosure would constitute a clearly unwarranted invasion of personal privacy), and the identity of undercover law enforcement officers. Other exemptions listed in the statute cover site files and records maintained by the Arkansas Historic Preservation Program and the Arkansas Archeological Survey; records relating to any Department of Health and Human Services risk or security assessment; unpublished drafts of judicial or quasi-judicial opinions and decisions; unpublished memoranda, working papers, and correspondence of the governor, members of the General Assembly, Supreme Court justices, and the attorney general; documents that are protected from disclosure by order or rule of court; and files that, if disclosed, would give advantage to competitors or bidders.

In 2009, the Arkansas General Assembly enacted several new exemptions to the Arkansas Freedom of Information Act. For example, Act 1291, which actually amended the Arkansas Freedom of Information Act (A.C.A. 25-19-105(b) – Exemptions), exempts concealed handgun licensee information; Act 393 amended the Trauma System Act (A.C.A. 20-13-80) by exempting "Any data, records, reports, and documents collected or compiled by or on behalf of the Department of Health, the Trauma Advisory Council, or other entity authorized under this subchapter for the purpose of quality or system assessment and improvement of the trauma system … to the extent that it identifies or could be used to identify any individual patient, provider, institution, or health plan; and Act 749 amended the Child Maltreatment Act (A.C.A. 12-18-101) by creating an exemption concerning the reporting of child maltreatment.

In 2011, the 20th exemption was added to the Arkansas FOIA. This one, included in Act 304, exempts from public access all prescription information submitted to the Department of Health under the state's new "Prescription Drug Monitoring Program." This program requires development of a statewide database that includes personal identifiers of those receiving controlled substances by prescription.

In addition to the exemptions listed in the Arkansas FOIA, at least 50 other statutory and regulatory exemptions to open government exist. As noted in the previous discussion of privacy invasion (see Chapter 4), many of these exemptions deal with personal information. Others, however, cover such diverse items as working papers of the Division of Legislative Audit; indictments issued against persons not in confinement; reports of physician misconduct submitted to the State Medical Board; birth certificates, death certificates, and other vital records held by the State Registrar; bank examination records filed with the State Bank Department; accident reports filed by drivers; and drivers' records held by the Office of Driver Services. Additional exemptions, embedded in other statutes, keep a variety of information from the public.

A new statutory exemption passed by the Arkansas General Assembly in 2009, Act 1366, amends a section of the Public Health and Welfare title (A.C.A. 20-78-106 – Availability of records of children's advocacy centers) and provides that records, correspondence, case histories, medical records, and other materials compiled by child advocacy centers are exempt from disclosure requirements.

Another act passed by the Arkansas General Assembly in 2009, Act 184, amends the Arkansas Freedom of Information Act (A.C.A. 25-19-107 – Exemptions) by requiring that all new statutory exemptions to the 1967 Act be specifically cross-referenced as exemptions to the act.

According to the Arkansas FOIA, custodians of records have a maximum of 24 hours to determine whether requested records are exempt from disclosure and to "... make efforts to the fullest extent possible to notify the person making the request and the subject of the records of that decision" (A.C.A. 25-19-105). This section continues, "Either the custodian, requester, or the subject of the records may immediately seek an opinion from the attorney general who, within three (3) working days of receipt of the request, shall issue an opinion stating whether the decision is consistent with this chapter." Attorney general opinions are not legally binding, and both the requester and subject of the records may seek judicial review of a custodian's decision.

For public records that are in active use or storage, the custodian must certify this fact in writing to the applicant and set a date and hour within three working days, at which time the record will be available for review and copying.

When custodians of records deny a citizen access to records, that citizen may appeal to the circuit court within his or her county of residence. The circuit court then has a maximum of seven days to hear and determine the case. If the circuit court finds that denial of access was unwarranted, it "... shall assess against the defendant reasonable attorney fees and other litigation expenses reasonably incurred by a plaintiff who has substantially prevailed unless ... other circumstances make an award of these expenses unjust" (A.C.A. 25-19-107). Fees and expenses may be assessed only against individual defendants (as opposed to the State of Arkansas or any of its agencies or departments), but they also may be assessed against a plaintiff who has initiated an action primarily for frivolous purposes or for purposes of delay.

Act 440, passed by the Arkansas General Assembly in 2009, also amends the Arkansas Freedom of Information Act (A.C.A. 25-19-107 – Appeal of denial of rights – Attorney's fees) and gives the State Claims Commission jurisdiction over claims for attorney's fees and other expenses incurred by plaintiffs who prevail in actions against state agencies under the Arkansas FOIA.

## Public Meetings

Public meetings are defined as "... the meetings of any bureau, commission, or agency of the state, or any political subdivision of the state, including municipalities and counties, boards of education, and all other boards, bureaus, commissions, or organizations in the State of Arkansas, except grand juries, supported wholly or in part by public funds or expending public funds" (A.C.A. 25-19-103).

In a decision handed down in October 2011, a Sebastian County circuit judge ruled that the Arkansas FOIA is unconstitutional in that it does not adequately define the term "meeting" (Harris v. City of Fort Smith). The issue arose as part of a lawsuit challenging the City of Fort Smith for making a series of informational one-on-one contacts to city directors concerning a hiring ordinance the city administrator planned to propose at an upcoming city directors meeting. The court ruled that "...an FOIA meeting cannot occur in the absence of at least two members of the subject governing body being present" (p. 44 of the opinion) and that "...the Arkansas FOIA, as applied, is overly broad and ... is determined to violate the Arkansas Constitution and the United States Constitution (p. 46 of the opinion). According to a newspaper story about this ruling, the decision is likely to be appealed (Hughes, 2011).

One section of the Arkansas FOIA provides that the time and place of each regular meeting shall be furnished to anyone who requests the information, and that in the event of emergency or special meetings, at least two hours before the meeting takes place the person calling the meeting must notify representatives of the media located in the county in which the meeting is to be held, as well as any news media located elsewhere that cover regular meetings of the governing body and that have requested to be notified of emergency or special meetings (A.C.A. 25-19-106).

This section also states that executive sessions are permitted only for the purpose of considering employment, appointment, promotion, demotion, disciplining, or resignation of any public officer or employee, but that such sessions must never be called for the purpose of defeating the reason or the spirit of the law. It continues, "No resolution, ordinance, rule, contract, regulation, or motion considered or arrived at in executive session will be legal unless, following the executive session, the public body reconvenes in public session and presents and votes on the resolution, ordinance, rule, contract, regulation, or motion."

Act 1445, passed by the Arkansas General Assembly in 2009, amends a section of the Education title (A.C.A. 6-18-507(d) – Suspension or expulsion of a public school student) by allowing public school boards to meet in executive session to consider appeals of the suspension or expulsion of a public school student, regardless of whether a parent or guardian requests a closed meeting.

As an addition to the Arkansas code governing public schools, Act 1588 of 2007 requires public school districts to post on their Web sites not less than 10 days prior to the date of a regular school board meeting a notice of the date, time, and place of that meeting (A.C.A. 6-13-619(a)); if a regular meeting is rescheduled, the district must post the change on its Web site not less than 24 hours prior to the rescheduled meeting.

Act 1302, passed by the Arkansas General Assembly in 2009,

amends a section of the State Government title (A.C.A. 25-19-219 – Publication on the Internet: Meeting dates) and requires each state agency to post at www.arkansas.gov the time and location of all public meetings held by the agency.

## Interpreting the Arkansas FOIA

A variety of court cases and literally hundreds of attorney general opinions have resulted from disagreements about the Freedom of Information Act. Because, as noted above, attorney general opinions are not legally binding, court decisions will be the main focus of interpretation.

While most of the early Arkansas Supreme Court decisions involving the Arkansas FOIA concerned questions about closed meetings, since 1981, most of the FOIA decisions have dealt with open records questions. The latter questions have involved both availability of records and costs to reproduce records.

### Open Records Cases

In one early records case, *McMahan v. Board of Trustees of the University of Arkansas* (1973), the court decided that the Arkansas FOIA did not provide that any particular records should be kept. At issue was a request for lists of people receiving complimentary tickets to in-state University of Arkansas football games, and the court said that such lists were not discoverable under the law.

In another athletics-related case, the court decided an issue involving information held by an intercollegiate athletic conference and its member schools (Arkansas Gazette Co. v. Southern State College, 1981). The newspaper publisher wanted to know the amount of money that member institutions dispersed to student athletes during the school year, but the organization and schools refused to disclose the information. In reversing the Pulaski County Circuit Court's judgment, the Arkansas Supreme Court noted that such information could not be classified as "educational records" and therefore it fell neither into the Arkansas FOIA scholastic exemption nor into the exemption created by the 1974 federal Family Education Rights and Privacy Act (20 U.S.C.A. 1232g (b)(1)). It also held that the records did not contain confidential information that would violate a student's reasonable expectation of privacy.

In one of several business-related FOIA cases, the court in 1988 held that the opinions of real estate appraisers, employed by the Arkansas Highway and Transportation Department to give appraisals of land the department needed to buy in order to construct a highway, were not exempt from disclosure (Arkansas Highway and Transportation Department v. Hope Brick Works, Inc.). Another aspect of the ruling in this case was that corporations were included in the intent of the Arkansas FOIA, and thus representatives of corporations should be afforded the same access to information received by any other citizen.

Two years later, the *Arkansas Gazette* requested from the Arkansas Industrial Development Commission a file containing the proposed location of a steel plant (Gannett River States Publishing v. Arkansas Industrial Development Commission, 1990). The court ruled that the lower court should review the file *in camera* (in the judge's chambers) to decide whether its contents fell within the "competitors" exemption. If it did not, the court said, then the file should be released.

In 1995, in another business-related case, the court ruled that a corporate application for a loan guarantee was exempt from the Arkansas FOIA (Byrne v. Eagle). At issue was information concerning a business that wanted to build a multi-purpose events center in North Little Rock. That same year, the court ruled that a hospital's quality assurance and peer review records were exempt from the Arkansas FOIA (Berry v. Saline Memorial Hospital).

Other records cases have involved questions about giving up records that either are not held by the agency or not created by the agency. In *Scott v. Smith* (1987), the court ruled that the Arkansas Department of Human Services had to give up documents held in the files of that agency's deputy general counsel and those agency documents which had been given to the assistant attorney general. In 1990, the *Springdale News* won a case in which the Arkansas Supreme Court ruled that the City of Fayetteville had to release memoranda prepared by outside counsel for the city, in connection with possible litigation over issuance of bonds (City of Fayetteville v. Edmark).

Five years later, in *Swaney v. Tilford* (1995), the court held that an auditor's working papers, prepared in connection with Arkansas Development Finance Authority audits, should be open to the public, even if the Development Finance Authority had to obtain them from a private custodian.

Questions about availability of police records also have reached the Arkansas Supreme Court. In 1988, the court ruled that once a federal indictment is returned, there no longer is an "undisclosed investigation," so police and fire department records related to the indictment should be open (City of Fayetteville v. Rose). One year later, in *McCambridge v. City of Little Rock* (discussed above in Chapter 4), the court held that the release of photographs and other details of an apparent murder-suicide, as well as copies of papers found in a briefcase at the crime scene, did not violate the privacy rights of the mother of one of the victims.

In two cases decided in 1990, the court ruled that investigative files of law enforcement agencies are exempt from disclosure (Martin v. Musteen; Arkansas Gazette Co. v. Goodwin). In the former case, even though an individual had been charged, the court felt that because the investigation was continuing and sensitive, the files should remain closed to the public. In the latter case, the court said the files could be closed to the public until after the trial had concluded.

In 1991, the court handed down a law enforcement records ruling with several implications (Hengel v. City of Pine Bluff). The case involved the public's right to inspect jail logs, arrest records, and shift sheets; staff members of the *Pine Bluff Commercial* sued the City of Pine Bluff and the police chief when they were refused access to those materials. The court ruled (1) that such records were subject to disclosure under the FOIA, (2) that it was a violation of the FOIA to black out information in the jail log, and (3) that the records should be available 24 hours a day, seven days a week because the Police Department was always open. This decision reinforced an earlier, unreported lower court decision in which the *Little River News* of Ashdown (Ark.) won access to all logbooks created by the Little River County Sheriff's Department (Sheriff's arrest records ruled open, 1985).

In *Young v. Rice* (1992), the court held that police department promotion records were exempt from disclosure under the personnel records exemption, and in 1994, the court ruled that law enforcement records concerning gang membership of potential witnesses in a murder trial were exempt from disclosure (Johninson v. Stodola).

Concerning the form in which records may be provided and the cost of copying such records, several cases have been decided. In

*Blaylock v. Staley* (1987), the court ruled that information on computer tapes is public record and the public is entitled to have access to that information in the form that it is kept. The court, however, also indicated that requests must be clear and that governmental agencies are not required to provide records in alternative formats.

This issue will become more prominent as alternative formats become more commonplace. Additionally, the issue concerning the release of software programs used in storing governmental data most likely will be resolved either by statute or by court decision in the near future, as many electronic records are of no use to the public when they are provided in an electronic format lacking the software to run them.

In 1996, in a case brought by an indigent prisoner, the Arkansas Supreme Court ruled that mere indigency does not entitle anyone to photocopies of public records at the public's expense (Moore v. State). The court said that in addition to indigency, there is a requirement to demonstrate a compelling need for such copies.

While the Arkansas FOIA states, "Reasonable access to public records and reasonable comforts and facilities for the full exercise of the right to inspect and copy those records shall not be denied to any citizen" (A.C.A. 25-19-105), a survey of governmental agencies found that fees for reproducing governmental documents were as high as $10 in some agencies (FOIA documents cost, 1996). A spokesperson for the Arkansas Attorney General's office has noted that one attorney general had established 25 cents as a reasonable charge for copying (McDonald, 1996).

In 2001, however, the General Assembly amended the Arkansas Freedom of Information Act to read as follows: "Except as provided in [A.C.A.] 25-19-109 or by law, any fee for copies shall not exceed the actual costs of reproduction, including the costs of the medium of reproduction, supplies, equipment, and maintenance, but not including existing agency personnel time associated with searching for, retrieving, reviewing, or copying the records." A.C.A. 25-19-109 is the section of the Arkansas Freedom of Information Act that provides for special requests for electronic information. This section of the law allows a custodian of electronic records to charge for verifiable costs of personnel time exceeding two hours, when the time is associated with the tasks of responding to the request.

Another records case to come before the Arkansas Supreme Court involved the definition of vital records, which are exempt from disclosure (Arkansas Department of Health v. Westark Christian Action, 1995). In that case, the court ruled that reports of aborted pregnancies were indeed vital records.

In a case decided by a lower court in April 1996, a Pulaski County Circuit Court judge ordered a defendant in a freedom of information case to pay the plaintiffs more than $10,000 in attorneys' fees (Dungan v. Johnson). According to a newspaper report of the case, it involved a request, by an *Arkansas Democrat-Gazette* reporter, for Correctional Medical Systems' manual outlining policies and procedures, because a prisoner in the Pulaski County jail had died and an employee of Correctional Medical Systems apparently was involved to some extent in decisions concerning the prisoner (Brummett, 1996).

Access to the manual was denied, so the reporter and the newspaper sued. Brummett reported that such a judgment was unprecedented, and that it far exceeded previous awards allowed by courts hearing FOIA cases.

Under A.C.A. 25-19-107, the Arkansas Supreme Court had ruled in 1998, plaintiffs are allowed to recover attorney's fees "...where public officials have acted arbitrarily or in bad faith in withholding records" (Burke v. Strange). In 2000, the Arkansas Court of Appeals awarded attorney's fees to a plaintiff who had been refused access to records held by the Beaverfork Fire Protection District (Kristen Investment Properties, LLC v. Faulkner County Waterworks and Sewer Public Facilities Board). The court in *Kristen* noted that a finding of arbitrary refusal or bad faith is not necessary in order for a trial court to award attorney's fees, for "... limiting the award of attorney's fees to only those cases involving a showing of bad faith or arbitrary conduct would be contrary to the liberal interpretation that we are to accord the FOIA and would defeat the intent of the General Assembly in enacting it" (72 Ark. App. 37 at 43).

In an unusual suit decided in 1998, the Arkansas Supreme Court ruled that the Arkansas Attorney General could sue Arkansas' Governor for access to records generated by a taxpayer-funded hot line (Bryant v. Weiss).

In April 2004, a Benton County Circuit Court judge ruled that because the Bentonville City Council's 2004 budget included money set aside for the Bentonville/Bella Vista Chamber of Commerce, and because the chamber had requested $8,000 in advertising from the local Advertising and Promotion Commission, the chamber's records were subject to the Arkansas Freedom of Information Act (See Roberts, S. (April 3, 2004). "Bentonville/Bella Vista chamber ruled subject to FOI." *Arkansas Democrat-Gazette,* Northwest Arkansas section, p. 13).

Also in 2004, the Arkansas Supreme Court ruled in *Nolan v. Little* that organic seed samples held by the Arkansas State Plant Board for testing were not public records under the Arkansas FOIA. A person had requested access to the seeds under the theory that they were available to the public under the FOIA.

In May 2007, in an unpublished three-sentence opinion, a Pulaski County circuit judge ruled that records of the Public Education Foundation of Little Rock, a private entity, fell under the Arkansas Freedom of Information Act. The plaintiff in the case argued that the Little Rock School District had financially supported the foundation, and thus it should be considered a public agency because it had been "funded wholly or in part by public funds," a phrase included as a cornerstone of the Arkansas Freedom of Information Act (Lynch, 2007).

In October 2007, the Arkansas Supreme Court ruled that e-mail messages sent to a Pulaski County computer were public records under the Arkansas FOIA (Pulaski County v. Arkansas Democrat-Gazette). The e-mail exchanges were between Ron Quillin, then the Pulaski County Comptroller, and a female representative from an out-of-state firm doing business with Pulaski County. The *Arkansas Democrat-Gazette* was denied the e-mails and sued to obtain them. Pulaski County and the firm's representative sought to keep them secret, in part because Pulaski County felt the trial court released the e-mails based on their overall context rather than on their content, and in part because the woman felt their release would violate her right to privacy, for they contained information about the romantic relationship that had developed between Quillin and the woman, including six graphic, sexually explicit photos. The Arkansas Supreme Court found that Pulaski County had not met its burden of proof that the lower court had not followed the 8th Circuit's earlier mandate to review the e-mails to determine if they constituted "... a record of the performance of official functions that are or should be carried out by a public official or employee," and that the woman waived her right of privacy when as a contractor with the county she sent e-mail messages to a county-owned computer.

## Open Meetings Cases

The first open meetings case to come before the Arkansas Supreme Court also was the first FOIA case to be heard by the court (Laman v. McCord, 1968). The case was brought against the North Little Rock City Council by the editor and managing editor of *THE Times of North Little Rock,* who believed the city council could not meet in closed session with its attorney. The court held that unless otherwise specifically provided by law, all meetings of governing bodies of municipalities shall be public meetings.

In 1975, *Arkansas Gazette* representatives went to court seeking to attend the University of Arkansas Board of Trustees' committee meetings (Arkansas Gazette Co. v. Pickens). Again, the court ruled in favor of the media.

One year later, the El Dorado Broadcasting Co. sued the mayor of El Dorado because the news media had been barred from meetings attended by the mayor, four of the city's eight aldermen, and the city's attorney (El Dorado Mayor v. El Dorado Broadcasting Co., 1976). The court ruled that even without a quorum, if city business was being discussed, the meetings must be open to the public. The Court noted that while the FOIA is inapplicable to "… a chance meeting or even a planned meeting of any two members of the city council," the FOIA does apply to "… any group meeting called by the mayor or any member of city council" (260 Ark at 824, 544 S.W. 2d at 208).

The media lost their first Arkansas Supreme Court meetings case in 1977, when the court ruled that an executive session of the Arkansas State Board of Corrections was exempt from the Arkansas FOIA (Commercial Printing Co. v. Rush). In this case, the *Pine Bluff Commercial* wanted access to a meeting in which board members were planning to discuss alleged wrongdoing by employees after an inmate had died. The court held that this was a personnel matter and, as such, was exempt under the FOIA. The justices did say, however, that a court could review *in camera* a tape of the meeting, to determine if the subject matter was exempt.

Also in 1977, the *Jonesboro Sun* and one of its reporters won an open meetings case, allowing the public to attend meetings between board members of the Jonesboro School District No. 1 and members of the North Central Association of Colleges and Schools (North Central Association of Colleges and Schools v. Troutt Brothers). An exceptionally important aspect of this ruling was the Arkansas Supreme Court's determination that meetings of any group expending public funds are open to the public, despite the dollar amount of those funds.

Four years later, the Arkansas Supreme Court decided a case involving a reporter, employed by Baxter County Newspapers, who wanted to prevent hospital personnel from going into executive session to discuss and vote on staff privileges in the hospital (Baxter County Newspapers v. Baxter General Hospital Staff, 1981). The court ruled that while discussion of the issue could be conducted in executive session, testimony and the vote should be taken in public.

In 1995, an open meetings question arose when representatives from a medical business wanted to attend meetings of the Arkansas Department of Human Services (National Park Medical Center v. Arkansas Department of Human Services). The staff meetings were being held to develop bid solicitations for medical service provider contracts, and the court ruled that the meetings could be closed to the public.

In a 2000 case involving a local school board meeting, an Arkansas circuit court judge ruled that the Valley View School District's school board had erred when it closed a meeting dealing with the suspension of a student (Associated Press, 2000). The *Jonesboro Sun* had challenged the action because state law provides for closed sessions only when a student has been expelled. "Under the law, a suspension from school does not exceed 10 days, and an expulsion exceeds 10 days" (p. 4B).

In 2004, the Arkansas Supreme Court decided a case in which the Fort Smith city administrator spoke individually with each of the Fort Smith City Board members and thereby gained approval to submit a bid to purchase real property at a price that would benefit taxpayers (Harris v. City of Fort Smith). The Court found that these serial one-on-one contacts constituted an informal board meeting subject to the FOIA.

As with opens records cases won by plaintiffs, attorney's fees have been an issue in open meetings cases as well. In 2006, a second suit by the plaintiff in *Harris v. City of Fort Smith* reached the Court. This time, Harris was asking for $10,000 in attorneys' fees because he had prevailed in the earlier case. The Court decided not to award Harris those fees because it felt the city officials had a laudable purpose for their actions and thus were substantially justified in secretly bidding for the property in question.

## Other Issues

Occasionally, after a court decision has been rendered, the Arkansas General Assembly passes legislation that essentially overturns that decision. This has happened several times in the area of freedom of information.

One example of this concerned disclosure of motor fuel tax records. In 1986, the court ruled that Department of Revenue records of motor fuel taxes collected from individuals were exempt from disclosure, but that such records of collections from businesses were not exempt because under the law, businesses had traditionally enjoyed less privacy protection than had individuals (Ragland v. Yeargan). In 1991, however, the General Assembly passed legislation opening many motor fuel tax records, including those of individuals (A.C.A. 26-18-303).

Another example occurred in 1987. In January, the court decided that *The Morning News of Northwest Arkansas* could have access to the working papers of auditors auditing the county circuit clerk's office (Legislative Joint Auditing Committee v. Woosley), but during its 1987 legislative session, the General Assembly exempted all such working papers from disclosure (A.C.A. 10-4-115 and A.C.A. 10-4-205).

Also, after the court in 1992 allowed reporters at the *Jonesboro Sun* access to the names of juveniles arrested on felony charges, but against whom no juvenile proceedings had yet been commenced (Trout Brothers v. Emison), the General Assembly in 1993 exempted this information from the FOIA (A.C.A. 9-27-352).

Act 332 of 1997, however, amending the Arkansas Code Annotated of 1987, Section 9-27-320, commands agencies to release to the general public the names, ages, and descriptions of juveniles committed or detained for offenses for which they could have been tried as adults, when such juveniles escape from either a youth service facility, the state hospital, or a juvenile detention facility.

In two other actions, the 81st General Assembly: 1) amended the Arkansas Freedom of Information Act to provide public access to most settlement agreements between state agencies and subjects of investigations against whom civil penalties were being sought (Act

873 of 1997) and 2) made public any contract entered into by any state agency (Act 1083 of 1997).

Another legislative action falling into the "other issues" category is Act 771, passed by the Arkansas General Assembly in 2009, amends a section of the Public Officers and Employees title (A.C.A. 21-1-503) and prevents public employees from taking adverse action as a result of public employees requesting records under the Arkansas FOIA.

# References

## Publications

Associated Press. (2000, July 7). Judge rules for newspaper in FOI lawsuit. *Arkansas Democrat-Gazette*, p. 4B.

Brummett, J. (1996, April 27). FOI law gains muscle. *Arkansas Democrat-Gazette*, p. 9B.

FOIA documents cost. (1996, December 5). *Arkansas Press Association Member Bulletin*, p. 5.

Hughes, D. (2011, Oct. 6). Appeals likely in ruling on open-meetings case. *Arkansas Democrat-Gazette*, p. 3B.

Lynch, J. (2007, May 25). Judge's ruling on foundation: Open records. *Arkansas Democrat-Gazette,* pp. B1, B10.

McDonald, T. (1996, December 29). Freedom of information designed to serve citizens. *Log Cabin Democrat*, p. 1A, 9A.

Roberts, S. (April 3, 2004). Bentonville/Bella Vista chamber ruled subject to FOI. *Arkansas Democrat-Gazette*, Northwest Arkansas section, p. 13.

Sheriff's arrest records ruled open, with limits. (1985, November 21). *Arkansas Gazette*, p. 2B.

## Cases

Arkansas Department of Health v. Westark Christian Action, 322 Ark. 440, 910 S.W.2d 199 (1995).

Arkansas Gazette Co. v. Goodwin, 304 Ark. 204, 801 S.W.2d 284 (1990).

Arkansas Gazette Co. v. Pickens, 258 Ark. 69, 522 S.W.2d 350 (1975).

Arkansas Gazette Co. v. Southern State College, 273 Ark. 248, 620 S.W.2d 258 (1981).

Arkansas Highway and Transportation Department v. Hope Brick Works, Inc., 294 Ark. 490, 744 S.W.2d 711 (1988).

Baxter County Newspapers v. Baxter General Hospital Staff, 273 Ark. 511, 622 S.W.2d 495 (1981).

Berry v. Saline Memorial Hospital, 322 Ark. 182, 907 S.W.2d 736 (1995).

Blaylock v. Staley, 293 Ark. 26, 732 S.W.2d 152 (1987).

Bryant v. Weiss, 335 Ark. 534, 983 S.W.2d 902 (1998).

Burke v. Strange, 335 Ark. 328, 983 S.W.2d 389 (1998).

Byrne v. Eagle, 319 Ark. 587, 892 S.W.2d 487 (1995).

City of Fayetteville v. Edmark, 304 Ark. 179, 801 S.W.2d 275 (1990).

City of Fayetteville v. Rose, 294 Ark. 468, 743 S.W.2d 817 (1988).

Commercial Printing Co. v. Rush, 261 Ark. 468, 549 S.W.2d 790 (1977).

Dungan v. Johnson, Pulaski County Circuit Court Case No. 95-9709 (1976).

El Dorado Mayor v. El Dorado Broadcasting Co., 260 Ark. 821, 544 S.W.2d 206 (1976).

Gannett River States Publishing v. Arkansas Industrial Development Commission, 303 Ark. 684, 799 S.W.2d 543 (1990).

Harris v. City of Fort Smith, 359 Ark. 355, 197 S.W.3d 461 (2004).

Harris v. City of Fort Smith, 366 Ark. 277, 234 S.W.3d 875 (2006).

Harris v. City of Fort Smith, CV-2009-935 (Oct. 4, 2011).

Hengel v. City of Pine Bluff, 307 Ark. 457, 821 S.W.2d 761 (1991).

Johninson v. Stodola, 316 Ark. 423, 872 S.W.2d 374 (1994).

Kristen Investment Properties, LLC v. Faulkner County Waterworks and Sewer Public Facilities Board, 72 Ark. App. 37, 32 S.W.3d 60 (2000).

Laman v. McCord, 245 Ark. 401, 432 S.W.2d 753 (1968).

Legislative Joint Auditing Committee v. Woosley, 291 Ark. 89, 722 S.W.2d 581 (1987).

Martin v. Musteen, 303 Ark. 656, 799 S.W.2d 540 (1990).

McCambridge v. City of Little Rock, 298 Ark. 219, 766 S.W.2d 909 (1989).

McMahan v. Board of Trustees of the University of Arkansas, 255 Ark. 108, 499 S.W.2d 56 (1973).

Moore v. State, 324 Ark. 453, 921 S.W.2d 606 (1996).

National Park Medical Center, Inc. v. Arkansas Department of Human Services, 322 Ark. 595, 911 S.W.2d 250 (1995).

Nolan v. Little, 359 Ark. 161, 196 S.W.3d 1 (2004).

North Central Association of Colleges and Schools v. Troutt Brothers, 261 Ark. 378, 548 S.W.2d 825 (1977).

Pulaski County v. Arkansas Democrat-Gazette, 371 Ark. 217, 264 S.W.3d 465 (2007).

Ragland v. Yeargan, 288 Ark. 81, 702 S.W.2d 23 (1986).

Scott v. Smith, 292 Ark. 174, 728 S.W.2d 515 (1987).

Swaney v. Tilford, 320 Ark. 652, 898 S.W.2d 462 (1995).

Troutt Brothers v. Emison, 311 Ark. 27, 841 S.W.2d 604 (1992).

Young v. Rice, 308 Ark. 593, 826 S.W.2d 252 (1992).

## Statutes and Court Rules

Administrative Order No. 6(c)(3) — Broadcasting, Recording, or Photographing in the Courtroom, A.C.A. Court Rules (1987).

Arkansas Open Checkbook Act, A.C.A 6-61-135 (1987).

Arkansas Financial Transparency Act, A.C.A. 25-1-40 (1987).

Child Maltreatment Act, A.C.A. 12-18-101 (1987).

Confidentiality of Records (Juvenile Arrest and Detention), A.C.A. 9-27-352 (1987).

Education: Suspension or expulsion of a public school student, A.C.A. 6-18-507(d) (1987).

Family Educational Rights and Privacy, 20 U.S.C. §1232g (b)(1) (2006).

Fingerprinting or Photographing (Juvenile Courts and Proceedings), A.C.A. 9-27-320 (1987).

Freedom of Information Act of 1967, A.C.A. 25-19-101 *et seq* (1987).

*In re* Adoption of Administrative Order No. 19 — Access to Case Records, A.C.A. 9-15-203 (1987).

Local Government: Electronic records, A.C.A. 14-14-111 (1987).

Public Health and Welfare: Availability of records of children's advocacy centers, A.C.A. 20-78-106 (1987).

Public Inspection—Filing of Certified Copies (Division of Legislative Audit), A.C.A. 10-4-205 (1987).

Public Officers and Employees, A.C.A. 21-1-503 (1987).

Records Confidential and Privileged—Exceptions (Motor Fuel Tax), A.C.A. 26-18-303 (1987)

Records—Public Inspection (Division of Legislative Audit), A.C.A. 10-4-115 (1987).

School Districts (Meetings), A.C.A. 6-13-619(a) (1987).

State Government: Administrative Procedures (Publication on the Internet – Meeting dates), A.C.A. 25-19-219 (1987).

Trauma System Act, A.C.A. 20-13-801 (1987).

Uniform Electronic Transactions Act, A.C.A. 25-32-101 *et seq.* (1987).

Chapter 7

# Media and the Courts

In the beginning of the 19th century, the U.S. Supreme Court began weighing the question as to whether jurors could be impartial if they knew something about the case before they became jurors. In fact, the modern-day Court in 1961 quoted an 1807 opinion by then Chief Justice John Marshall, who had written, "[L]ight impressions, which may fairly be supposed to yield to the testimony offered, which leave the mind open to a fair consideration of that testimony, constitute no sufficient objection to a juror" (Irvin v. Dowd, 366 U.S. at 722, note 3). This was of concern because the Sixth Amendment to the U.S. Constitution, ratified in 1791, guarantees defendants a speedy and public trial by an impartial jury.

Nearly a century and half later, the Court overturned a rape conviction of three black defendants on the basis that blacks had been excluded from the jury, but more importantly for the media, the Court said that prejudicial news coverage of the case had been a more significant obstruction to justice than had the jury selection process (Shepherd v. Florida, 1951). The observation was a hint of things to come.

Eight years later, in *Marshall v. United States* (1959), the Court said jurors could not be impartial after having read two newspaper stories about the prior convictions of two defendants, and two years after that the Court for the first time reversed a state criminal conviction solely on grounds of prejudicial pre-trial publicity (Irvin v. Dowd, 1961).

Although there are no laws that prohibit the media from writing stories about crime and the trials that follow crime, states have taken steps to reduce publicity about certain types of judicial proceedings of both criminal and civil natures. While recognizing the value of public hearings and trials, Arkansas is among those states that have selectively attempted to balance free expression rights with privacy rights and with the right to a trial by an impartial jury.

One attempt to do so is a guarantee contained in Article 2, Sec. 10 of the Arkansas Constitution, which reads, "In all criminal prosecutions the accused shall enjoy the right to a speedy and public trial by an impartial jury of the county in which the crime shall have been committed ..." (1874). Other attempts are contained in state statutes.

## Statutes and Rules

As noted above, the Arkansas Constitution guarantees a public trial. Additionally, a state statute reinforces this notion, reading, "The sittings of every court shall be public, and every person may freely attend the sittings of every court" (A.C.A. 16-10-105). There are, however, exceptions.

Concerning pre-trial proceedings, one statute reads, "Upon the request of the defendant, all persons may be excluded from the room in which the examination is made except the magistrate, his clerk, the peace officer, the prosecutor, the attorney or attorneys representing the state, the prisoner, his counsel, and the witnesses under examination" (A.C.A. 16-85-204).

Also, Arkansas Code Annotated of 1987, Section 16-13-318, states, "The chancery courts of the various judicial districts of the state shall, upon application of all litigants to a divorce action, proceeding for alimony or separate maintenance, proceeding touching the maintenance or custody of children, proceeding for annulment of marriage, adoption proceeding, or any other proceeding pertaining to domestic relations, hear the case or matter in privacy."

Juvenile court records, too, are generally closed to the public, although all records may be closed and confidential within the discretion of the court (A.C.A. 9-27-309). As noted in Chapter 6, adoption hearings and records are confidential (A.C.A. 9-9-217), as are juvenile arrest and detention records (A.C.A. 9-27-352), unless the juvenile escapes from custody after being committed or detained for an offense for which he or she could have been tried as an adult (A.C.A. 9-27-320, as amended by Act 332 of 1997).

When any person violates the confidentiality of a court proceeding or, more precisely, if there is willful resistance by any person to the lawful order or process of the court, that person may be subject to criminal contempt and a fine of up to $50 or imprisonment for no more than 10 days, or both (A.C.A. 16-10-108). Contempt also may be committed through disorderly, contemptuous, or insolent behavior during the court's sitting or by any breach of the peace, noise, or disturbance directly tending to interrupt court proceedings.

Finally, as a remedy to pre-trial publicity that undermines the guarantee of an impartial jury, Arkansas law allows for one change of venue (A.C.A. 16-88-203), and allows that "Any criminal cause pending in any circuit court may be removed by the order of the court ... to the circuit court of another county whenever it shall appear ... that the minds of the inhabitants of the county in which the cause is pending are so prejudiced against the defendant that a fair and impartial trial cannot be held in that county" (A.C.A. 16-88-201).

To help determine that an impartial jury is impaneled in a criminal trial, counsel for the State and for the defendant may exercise a limited number of challenges to potential jurors without cause (called peremptory challenges). In Arkansas, counsel for the State may exercise ten, six, and three peremptory challenges in capital murder cases, other felonies, and misdemeanors, respectively, while counsel for the defendant may exercise twelve, eight, and three peremptory challenges, respectively, in such cases (A.C.A. 16-33-305).

While courtrooms are "presumptively open" (A.C.A. 16-10-105), a court reporter's transcript of an open proceeding is not a public record. A court reporter shall make a transcript upon request of a judge or a party. A record may not be prepared upon request of a third party, such as the press (A.C.A. 16-13-510).

One other issue relating both to publicity and to the guarantee of a public trial is whether trials may be broadcast, recorded, and photographed. In 1980, the Arkansas Supreme Court agreed to permit a one-year experiment allowing broadcasting and photographing of trials, with the exception of juvenile court proceedings (*Re* Petition of Arkansas Bar Association, 1980). The experiment was to run during 1981.

In 1982, a committee created to examine the effects of cameras in courtrooms during trials recommended that cameras should be allowed to remain in court, with the exception that if a party to the case objects at the beginning of the trial, then cameras would be removed. The Arkansas Supreme Court agreed (*In re* Modification of the Code of Judicial Conduct, 1982). Currently, Administrative Order

Number 6 of the Arkansas Court Rules (1996) governs broadcasting, recording, and photographing in court.

The order, which applies to all courts (including appellate courts) except the juvenile division of chancery court, states that a judge may authorize broadcasting, recording, or photographing in the courtroom, but that a timely objection by a party or an attorney shall preclude such activity. Witnesses may refuse to be taped or photographed, and there is to be no camera activity involving jurors, minors without parental or guardian consent, victims in cases involving sexual offenses, and undercover police agents or informants.

Effective Aug. 1, 2011, the Arkansas Supreme Court now prohibits the recording and broadcasting of drug-court proceedings, thus amending its Administrative Order No. 6. Although such courts had involved minors and had allowed taping and broadcasting of proceedings since at least 2004, the Court noted in its Revised Order that it had concerns about matters of privacy and the potential for abuse of broadcast recordings (*In re* Administrative Order No. 6(c), 2011 Ark. 317).

The order also requires that media representatives enter into a pooling arrangement in which they share tapes, films, and photographs. The media pool may have one still camera and one television camera in the courtroom, but additional videotaping equipment and electronic equipment must be located outside the courtroom. No artificial lighting device is allowed, film changes may not be made while court is in session, and equipment must be removed when court is not in session.

In 1993, Administrative Order Number 6 was amended to include a section concerning contempt. It reads, "Failure to abide by any provision of this Order can result in a citation for contempt against the news representative and his or her agency."

Administrative Order No. 6 also provides that the Supreme Court and Court of Appeals may make their proceedings available by audio or video recording. The Courts have begun to implement that provision by creating a Streaming Media Archive of their oral arguments. The archive is available at the Arkansas Judiciary Web site: *https://courts.arkansas.gov.*

Two Acts passed by the 86th General Assembly in 2007 amended existing law concerning 1) juror confidentiality and 2) dissemination of criminal history information. Act 226, among other things, amended

A.C.A. 16-32-1 to make confidential any juror information submitted to a circuit court or circuit clerk from which the identity of a particular juror can be determined. Juror information is defined as a list of potential jurors; a list of potential jurors who were sworn and qualified; any response to a juror questionnaire; and a list of an individual venire panel.

Act 59 amended A.C.A. 12-12-1503(2) to exclude from the definition of "arrest records" felony arrest information if more than three years have elapsed from the date of the felony arrest. This could make it more difficult for journalists and others to determine patterns of felony arrests for serial criminals. The statute already had excluded misdemeanor arrest information, as well as felony arrest information that had a disposition of acquittal, dismissal, or *nolle prosequi* entered into the central repository.

## Judicial Remedies for Media Publicity

Judges in trial courts have at their disposal several remedies for media publicity. Some remedies are more extreme than others, with perhaps the most extreme being to place a restrictive order on the media, preventing them from publishing certain information before the trial begins. Such orders, commonly known as "gag" orders, require sufficient proof that they will indeed prevent a clear and present danger of media content contaminating the jury pool so extensively that an impartial jury cannot be found.

Guidelines for placing restrictive orders on the media were created by the U.S. Supreme Court in a 1976 decision involving the issue. At that time, the Court said such orders should be considered in light of (a) the nature and extent of pre-trial news coverage; (b) whether other measures would be likely to mitigate the effects of unrestrained pre-trial publicity; and (c) how effectively a restraining order would operate to prevent the threatened danger (Nebraska Press Association v. Stuart).

In ruling against the restrictive order at issue, the Court indicated that for a restrictive order to be valid, intense and pervasive publicity concerning the case should be certain, no other judicial remedy would mitigate the effects of pre-trial publicity, and the restrictive order would in fact effectively prevent prejudicial material from reaching potential jurors.

As a less extreme alternative to gagging the media, courts may ask attorneys and other officers of the court, law enforcement officers, witnesses, and jurors not to talk to the media about the case. While perhaps not as effective as a restrictive order on the media, it clearly saves the court from violating the media's First Amendment rights.

Another extreme remedy to mitigate media publicity is to close the courtroom to the public. Although criminal trials may be closed only under extreme circumstances (e.g., young or frightened witnesses, disclosure of secret information, witness is undercover agent), civil trials, with the consent of both parties, may be closed in Arkansas at a judge's discretion. Barring the press from pre-trial hearings, though also extreme, is much more recognized by courts than barring the press from trials. In fact, in some states (California, for example), if a defendant requests that the press be barred from pre-trial hearings, it must be done.

Less extreme remedies include changes of venue, changes of venire, and sequestering juries. A change of venue may be expensive for the court, and there is no guarantee that prejudicial publicity will not follow the trial to the locale to which it is moved. A change of venire, referring to the process of bringing in jurors from another locale where pre-trial publicity may not have been so extreme, also may be expensive and may cause juror backlash against defendants. Similarly, sequestering jurors (keeping them apart from the public during the trial) may be costly for the court and may cause juror backlash against defendants.

If the above-mentioned remedies are not feasible or appropriate, granting a pre-trial continuance (postponement) may help until the publicity dies down, but there is no guarantee that such publicity will not return when the trial resumes. It also means that a defendant may not receive a constitutionally guaranteed speedy trial. In addition, during a continuance, witnesses may forget details related to their testimony, and some witnesses may move away or die.

As part of jury selection, another remedy is extensive *voir dire*, which places responsibility on attorneys to select jurors who have not been affected by media publicity. After jury selection, a judge may admonish jurors not to discuss the case with anyone and not to pay attention to any media reports related to the case. Both of these remedies are less drastic than others, but they may not be as effective.

When more than one defendant is accused of the same or a related crime, defendants may be tried separately, to reduce the influence of media publicity received by any given defendant. Trying co-defendants separately is called severance.

Ultimately, when defendants believe their trial outcome have been contaminated by media publicity, they can appeal the verdicts to a higher court. This, of course, is not a better remedy than preventing the true effects of pre-trial publicity, but it is a safety net for times when other remedies have failed.

## Cases

The most frequently litigated questions involving the media and the judiciary in Arkansas have concerned media publicity and its effects on jurors. In dealing with this conflict, the Arkansas Supreme Court made a definitive statement in a 1955 decision that upheld convictions for robbery and burglary (Rowe v. State). In part, the defendant complained that some members of the jury pool had formed tentative opinions based upon newspaper reports of the crimes, but the court ruled there was no error in accepting jurors who had stated they could and would be guided solely by the testimony. The court said, "It is no longer practicable in an intelligent society to select jurors from a psychological vacuum or from a stratum where information common to the community as a whole is lacking" (224 Ark. at 673; 275 S.W.2d at 888).

Despite this sentiment, in the decades to follow there were numerous requests from defendants, based upon pre-trial publicity, that the Arkansas Supreme Court require venue changes or overturn convictions. Sometimes the court agreed. For example, in 1964, the court ruled that even though a trial had to be moved to a different judicial district, a change of venue was warranted because of pre-trial publicity (Cockrell v. Dobbs).

Fourteen years later, the conviction in the highly publicized capital murder trial of John Edward Swindler, who had been convicted of murdering a Fort Smith police officer, was reversed because the trial had not been moved to another county, and the *voir dire* procedure had shown there was much juror knowledge of the crime (Swindler v. State, 1978). The court said the "... proper test is whether a juror can lay aside his impression or opinion and render a verdict based upon evidence presented in court" (264 Ark. at 114; 569 S.W.2d at 124). A year later, Swindler claimed he should have been granted a second change of venue, but both the Arkansas Supreme Court and the U.S. Supreme Court disagreed (Swindler v. State, 1979).

In another highly publicized capital murder case, the convictions of two defendants were reversed because the defendants had not been granted a change of venue (Ruiz v. State, 1979). Ruiz and his co-defendant were convicted again and sentenced to death, but they appealed two more times, claiming media publicity still had prevented them from gaining a fair trial. Both times, the Arkansas Supreme Court disagreed (Ruiz v. State, 1981; Ruiz v. State, 1989).

In 1980, the court ruled that a change of venue was not required merely because jurors had read newspaper accounts of the crime before becoming jurors (Matthews v. State). In 1982, the court refused a second change of venue for a defendant who had been convicted of murder, although the defendant claimed that jurors had been prejudiced by media coverage of the murders (Perry v. State). Two years later, Mary Lee Orsini, after a much-publicized murder trial in Pulaski County Circuit Court, asked the Arkansas Supreme Court to overturn her conviction because of pre-trial publicity that she claimed had prejudiced the jurors (Orsini v. State, 1984). The court, noting that jurors had been examined for prejudice in the judge's chambers, declined to do so, as did the U.S. Supreme Court.

In *Gardner v. State* (1988), the issue of pre-trial publicity was raised at the Arkansas Supreme Court after the defendant was convicted of committing two murders in Fort Smith. The trial court had refused Gardner a change of venue, and the higher court upheld Gardner's conviction. In its decision, the Arkansas Supreme Court noted the following types of media coverage of the case: (1) the murder investigation was a lead story on the day the crime was discovered and possibly one or two days thereafter, and (2) subsequently, the news media broadcast pictures of Gardner; items found on Gardner and speculation that they had been taken from the murder scene; statements Gardner made to a bus station employee that he had killed a woman and taken her jewelry; and Gardner's criminal record from another state as well as information that he was on parole from prison. Citing *Swindler v. State* (1978), the court reiterated, "... it is not necessary that jurors be totally ignorant of the facts surrounding the case ...." (296 Ark. at 52; 754 S.W.2d at 523).

In two other cases, the Arkansas Supreme Court also has affirmed its faith in the *voir dire* process as a way to ensure an impartial jury (Bussard v. State, 1989; Bell v. State, 1996). In both cases, the court held that *voir dire* provided adequate safeguards against pretrial publicity.

## Access to Proceedings

The second most frequently litigated area concerning media and the judiciary involves access to court proceedings. In a 1977 case, the Arkansas Supreme Court ruled that the press and the public should not have been excluded from the *voir dire* process, even though the defense counsel had asked the judge to conduct the process in chambers (Commercial Printing Co. v. Lee). The court implied that members of the press should have complained about being excluded before the process was completed.

In another case involving access to *voir dire*, the court reversed a variety of criminal convictions of a single defendant because *voir dire* was held in chambers, with the public excluded (Taylor v. State, 1984). Noting that defendants are entitled to public trials, the court reiterated that the public and the press may insist upon criminal trials being open to everyone.

Ten years later, the court ruled that jury selection in general should be open to the public (Memphis Publishing Co. v. Burnett, 1994). Citing *Arkansas Department of Human Services v. Hardy* (1994), the court said that jury selection is a stage of the proceedings where openness is particularly appropriate under the guarantee of a public trial.

In addition to dealing with access to jury selection, the court has dealt with access to suppression hearings. In 1979, the Arkansas Supreme Court ruled that the media and the public should not be excluded from suppression hearings that are held without the jury present (Shiras v. Britt). In this case, a reporter for the *Arkansas Gazette* had refused the trial judge's offer to let her stay at the hearing if she agreed to submit (for censorship purposes) anything she wrote about evidence discussed at the hearing. The trial judge then asked her to leave, she and the Arkansas Gazette Co. asked the higher court to overrule the trial court, and the higher court agreed.

Four years later, events in the highly publicized Barry Lee Fairchild murder case led to another decision about suppression hearings (Arkansas Television Co. v. Tedder, 1983). In this case, the trial judge closed a hearing to ensure selection of an impartial jury, which he said he thought would be virtually impossible if the confession was reported. Owners of a Little Rock TV station appealed this decision, and the Arkansas Supreme Court ruled that to overcome the presumption of open pre-trial hearings, there must be demonstrated a substantial probability that "(1) irreparable damage to the defendant's fair trial right will result from an open hearing, and (2) alternatives to closure will not adequately protect the right to a fair trial" (281 Ark. at 156; 662 S.W.2d at 176).

The presumption of open pre-trial hearings also applies to juveniles being tried as adults. In 1984, the Arkansas Supreme Court ruled that without a showing of irreparable harm to the defendant's right to a fair trial, a lower court erred in closing a pre-trial hearing of a 15-year-old boy charged with capital murder (Arkansas Newspaper, Inc. v. Patterson, 1984).

## Contempt Issues

In another area relating to media—contempt judgments—the Arkansas Supreme Court has handed down several rulings involving publications. The first such ruling occurred in 1855, after publication of a newspaper article in the *Des Arc Citizen* criticized the Arkansas Supreme Court's motives and attributed one of its decisions to extraneous influences, which the court took to mean bribery (State v. Morrill). When the publisher was summoned to respond to contempt considerations, he challenged the court's authority over his actions outside of court. He also said that if the court needed a further answer, he would swear that it hadn't been his intention to impugn the court and that he had been unfortunate in the selection of language and the construction of his sentences.

The court continued the case into the next year and then accepted the publisher's statement that he had not meant to imply that the court had fallen victim to bribery. In fact, before he had been summoned to court, the publisher had published a statement to that effect. The court believed him and dropped the case, but not before it emphasized that the Arkansas Constitution granted it the authority to punish with contempt charges those persons who abused the liberty of the press through libelous publications (16 Ark. at 402).

Nearly 100 years later, publishers of the *Arkansas State Press*, a weekly newspaper serving Arkansas' black community, were held in contempt for publishing an article headlined, "Strikers Sentenced to Pen by Hand-Picked Jury" (Bates v. State, 1946). The article criticized a judge's handling of a trial in which three strikers were convicted of preventing another worker from engaging in a lawful occupation. Among other things that irritated the judge, the article said, "The prosecution was hard-pressed to make a case until Judge Lawrence C. Auten instructed the jury that the pickets could be found guilty if they aided or assisted, or just stood idly by while violence occurred" (210 Ark. at 654; 197 S.W.2d at 47).

The Arkansas Supreme Court weighed the question of whether or not the article tended to interfere with orderly conduct of the judiciary, and it decided that such comment did not create a clear and present danger to the administration of justice. It therefore dismissed contempt charges against Christopher (known as L.C.) and Daisy Bates, the publishers.

In 1962, contempt charges were brought against a person who had distributed 2,300 copies of a pamphlet titled, "Inside Information About Wrong Doings of Election Commissioners and County Judge of Newton County, Arkansas" (Tupy v. State). The contempt charges were upheld because the pamphlet's publisher was found to have destroyed public confidence in the courts and in grand juries by, in effect, charging "... that he [could not] obtain justice in a court of Newton County because of a rigged Grand Jury engineered by the Circuit Court" (234 Ark. at 825; 354 S.W.2d at 730). The court said this created a clear and present danger to the administration of justice.

Another interesting case concerning a contempt charge against the media involved the executive editor of the *Texarkana Gazette* (Wood v. Goodson, 1972). The facts of the case were that during concurrent rape trials with different juries, one jury reached a verdict, and the judge asked the *Gazette's* court reporter not to print the verdict in the next morning's paper. That evening, the paper's executive editor called the judge to say he wasn't going to honor the request, so the judge withdrew the request and made it an order. The judge did say that the verdict could be printed in the afternoon edition or in other editions.

Despite the order, the jury verdict was published in a story placed prominently on the front page of the next morning's paper. The executive editor was held in contempt, and he appealed. The Arkansas Supreme Court vacated the contempt judgment and stated, "No court ... has the power to prohibit the news media from publishing that which transpires in open court" (253 Ark. at 203; 485 S.W.2d at 217).

In May 2000, a Washington County judge ordered the news media not to publish the name or photographs of a juvenile or of certain other key figures in an attempted capital murder case. Although the judge narrowed the gag order two days later, she held the *Arkansas Democrat-Gazette* in contempt of court for violating the modified order by publishing photographs of the juvenile and his parents.

The newspaper, along with a variety of other media organizations, appealed the gag order. In June, the Arkansas Supreme Court ruled 6-0 that the gag order was an unconstitutional prior restraint on the press, describing it as a "plain, manifest, clear and gross abuse of discretion" (*Arkansas Democrat-Gazette* v. Zimmerman, 2000). On July 24, 2000, Judge Zimmerman dropped her finding of contempt against the *Arkansas Democrat-Gazette* (Davis, 2000).

In 2006, the Arkansas Supreme Court in *The Helena Daily World v. Simes* reversed a gag order entered by Phillips County Circuit Judge L.T. Simes II against *The Helena Daily World*. The order prevented *The Helena Daily World* from publishing testimony given in an open proceeding that sought the judge's recusal in a case. The Helena mayor had testified about a complaint filed against the judge with the Arkansas Judicial and Disability Commission. Because Arkansas law makes such investigations confidential until concluded, Judge Simes entered the gag order to prevent any reference to the testimony. Citing the *Zimmerman* decision, the Court ruled that a statute cannot authorize a violation of the First Amendment. "Once [the Mayor] gave his testimony in open court, the [Judge] could not undo what had been done by attempting to suppress testimony after the fact" (365 Ark. at 312; 229 S.W.3d at 5).

## Cameras in the Courtroom

In addition to the controversies described above, a final media issue to arise in court concerns cameras in the courtroom, and three cases in the 1980s dealt with this question. The first involved a defense objection to television and other media coverage of the sentencing stage of a trial, but the Arkansas Supreme Court ruled that the objection came too late in the trial (Ford v. State, 1982). In that same year, the court ruled that broadcasters do not have an absolute right to cover a trial (KARK-TV v. Lofton). In this case, the defendant's objection to a TV camera in the courtroom was sustained because the objection was made before the trial started.

Oddly, in another case heard two years later by the Arkansas Supreme Court, the court did not overturn a defendant's conviction based on the fact that the trial judge allowed a trial to be recorded and photographed, despite the defendant's objection to such coverage at the beginning of the trial (Jim Halsey Co., Inc. v. Bonar, 1984). The judge had ruled that if the coverage became a distraction, the photographer and recorder would be removed if the defense objected again, but the defense did not object a second time.

# References

## Publications

Davis, A. (2000, July 25). Judge drops her finding of contempt. *Arkansas Democrat-Gazette*, p. 1B, 3B.

## Cases

Arkansa Democrat-Gazette v. Zimmerman, 341 Ark. 771, 20 S.W.3d 301 (2000).

Arkansas Department of Human Services v. Hardy, 316 Ark. 119, 871 S.W.2d 352 (1994).

Arkansas Newspaper, Inc. v. Patterson, 281 Ark. 213, 662 S.W.2d 826 (1984).

Arkansas Television Co. v. Tedder, 281 Ark. 152, 662 S.W.2d 174 (1983).

Bates v. State, 210 Ark. 652, 197 S.W.2d 45 (1946).

Bell v. State, 324 Ark. 258, 920 S.W.2d 821 (1996).

Bussard v. State, 300 Ark. 174, 778 S.W.2d 213 (1989).

Cockrell v. Dobbs, 238 Ark. 348, 381 S.W.2d 756 (1964).

Commercial Printing Co. v. Lee, 262 Ark. 87, 553 S.W.2d 270 (1977).

Ford v. State, 276 Ark. 98, 633 S.W.2d 3 (1982).

Gardner v. State, 296 Ark. 41, 754 S.W.2d 518 (1988).

Helena Dailey World v. Simes, 365 Ark. 305, 229 S.W. 3d 1 (2006).

Irvin v. Dowd, 366 U.S. 717 (1961).

Jim Halsey Co., Inc. v. Bonar, 284 Ark. 461, 683 S.W.2d 898, *rehearing denied*, 285 Ark. 461, 688 S.W.2d 275 (1985).

KARK-TV v. Lofton, 277 Ark. 228, 640 S.W.2d 798 (1982).

Marshall v. United States, 360 U.S. 310 (1959).

Matthews v. State, 268 Ark. 484, 598 S.W.2d 58 (1980).

Memphis Publishing Co. v. Burnett, 316 Ark. 176, 871 S.W.2d 359 (1994).

Nebraska Press Association v. Stuart, 427 U.S. 539 (1976).

Orsini v. State, 281 Ark. 348, 665 S.W.2d 245, *cert. denied*, 469 U.S. 847 (1984).

Perry v. State, 277 Ark. 357, 641 S.W.2d 865 (1982).

Rowe v. State, 224 Ark. 671, 275 S.W.2d 887 (1955).

Ruiz v. State, 265 Ark. 875, 582 S.W.2d 915 (1979).

Ruiz v. State, 273 Ark. 94, 617 S.W.2d 6 (1981).

Ruiz v. State, 299 Ark. 144, 772 S.W.2d 297 (1989).

Shepherd v. Florida, 341 U.S. 50 (1951).

Shiras v. Britt, 267 Ark. 97, 589 S.W.2d 18 (1979).

State v. Morrill, 16 Ark. 384 (1855).

Swindler v. State, 264 Ark. 107, 569 S.W.2d 120 (1978).

Swindler v. State, 267 Ark. 418, 592 S.W.2d 91 (1979), *cert. denied*, 449 U.S. 1057 (1980).

Taylor v. State, 248 Ark. 103, 679 S.W.2d 797 (1984).

Tupy v. State, 234 Ark. 821, 354 S.W.2d 728 (1962).

Wood v. Goodson, 253 Ark. 196, 485 S.W.2d 213 (1972).

## Constitutions, Statutes, and Court Rules

Administrative Order Number 6 — Broadcasting, Recording, or Photographing in the Courtroom, A.C.A. Court Rules (1987).

Arkansas Constitution, Article 2, Section 10 (Speedy and Public Trial, Impartial Jury) (1874).

Challenges to Jurors, A.C.A. 16-33-305 (1987).

Confidentiality of Records (Juvenile Courts), A.C.A. 9-27-309 (1987).

Confidentiality of Records (Juvenile Arrest and Detention), A.C.A. 9-27-351 (1987).

Confidentiality of Hearings and Records (Adoption), A.C.A. 9-9-217 (1987).

Contempt, A.C.A. 16-10-108 (1987).

Crime Reporting and Investigations (Definitions), A.C.A. 12-12-1503(2) (1987).

Exclusion of Persons from Courtroom, A.C.A. 16-85-204 (1987).

Fingerprinting or Photographing (Juvenile Courts and Proceedings), A.C.A. 9-27-320 (1987).

*In re* Modification of the Code of Judicial Conduct, 275 Ark. 495, 628 S.W.2d 573 (1982).

One Change of Venue, A.C.A. 16-88-203 (1987).

Private Hearings by Chancery Courts, A.C.A. 16-13-318 (1987).

Re Petition of Arkansas Bar Association, 271 Ark. 358, 609 S.W.2d 28 (1980).

Removal for Prejudice (Change of Venue), A.C.A. 16-88-201 (1987).

Selection and Attendance (General Provisions), A.C.A. 16-32-1 (1987).

Sittings of Courts to be Public, A.C.A. 16-10-105 (1987).

Chapter 8

# Obscenity

The history of Arkansas obscenity law began in 1837, when Arkansas passed its first obscenity statute. Rommel (1994) provided a thorough description of the evolution of such statutes, noting that the first one focused primarily on public nudity and the exhibition of obscene or indecent pictures and figures, but contained neither a definition of obscenity nor a prohibition against the sale of obscene materials (p. 398).

## Statutes and Ordinances

Current state law, with its origins in 1947, has been amended frequently during legislative sessions and now contains portions that apply to all forms of electronic communications (A.C.A. Title 5, Chapts. 68 (Obscenity) and 27 (Offenses Against Children)). In addition to prohibiting nudism as a social practice (A.C.A. 5-68-204), the law contains individual sections prohibiting the sale or possession of literature rejected by the U.S. mails (A.C.A. 5-68-202); making it unlawful for any person to knowingly exhibit, sell, offer to sell, give away, circulate, produce, distribute, attempt to distribute, or have in his or her possession any obscene film (A.C.A. 5-68-203); and prohibiting public displays of obscenity (A.C.A. 5-68-205).

It also contains a section that defines obscene material according to the U.S. Supreme Court's definition in *Miller v. California* (1973), incorporating the following three-pronged test:

(a) depicts or describes in patently offensive manner sadomas ochistic abuse, sexual conduct, or hard-core sexual conduct;

(b) taken as a whole, appeals to the prurient interest of the aver age person, applying contemporary statewide standards; and

(c) taken as a whole, lacks serious literary, artistic, political, or scientific value (A.C.A. 5-68-302).

Other sections make it illegal to promote obscene materials (including the idea of possessing obscene material with the intent to promote) (A.C.A. 5-68-303); to promote an obscene performance or commit an obscene performance at a live public show (A.C.A. 5-68-304 and 305); to publicly display obscene material for advertising purposes (A.C.A. 5-68-306); and to possess, sell, or distribute both mailable and nonmailable material (A.C.A. 5-68-404 and 405). Oddly, the law contains a section stating that possession of prohibited materials, except for the purpose of returning them to the person from whom they were received, creates a presumption that the materials are intended for sale or commercial distribution, exhibition, or gift (A.C.A. 5-68-415). This section does, however, note that the presumption shall be rebuttable, but that the burden of proof is on the person possessing the materials.

Fortunately, employees of motion picture theaters who neither own nor manage the theaters (and who have no say in the selection of movies shown in the theaters) are not liable to prosecution for showing obscene films (A.C.A. 5-68-308). Additionally, employees, directors, and trustees of bona fide schools, museums, and public libraries, acting within the scope of their regular employment, also are exempt from prosecution for disseminating writings, films, slides, drawings, or other visual reproductions which are claimed to be obscene.

Arkansas law also makes it illegal to sell or to loan pornography to minors, defined as people under age 17 (A.C.A. 5-68-501), or to sexually exploit children (A.C.A. 5-27-301 *et seq.*), defined as people under age 17 (A.C.A. 5-27-302). This includes the use of children in any sexual performance, defined as "... any play, dance, act, drama, piece, interlude, pantomime, show, scene, or other three-dimensional presentation or parts thereof whether performed live or photographed, filmed, videotaped, or visually depicted by any other photographic, cinematic, magnetic, or electronic means" (A.C.A. 5-27-401). The latter portion of this section could mean that animated and computer-generated depictions of children may not be portrayed in sexual situations. In a 6-3 decision in 2002, the U.S. Supreme Court in *Ashcroft v. Free Speech Coalition* struck down a federal law that banned virtual depiction of child pornography. This means that the Arkansas law prohibiting similar electronic depictions could not be legally enforced.

Subsequent sections of the law protecting children also prohibit anyone from pandering or possessing visual or print media depicting sexually explicit conduct involving a child (A.C.A. 5-27-304); from employing or consenting to use children in a sexual performance (A.C.A. 5-27-402); and from producing, directing, or promoting the sexual performance of children (A.C.A. 5-27-403). Defendants facing charges of violating these two sections may offer as a defense their good faith, reasonable belief that the person who engaged in the sexual conduct was 17 years of age or older (A.C.A. 5-27-404).

An Internet service provider, including news Web sites and forums, has no criminal liability under Arkansas child pornography statutes when it is the "intermediary between the sender and receiver" of child pornographic images (A.C.A. 5-27-608). An ISP, however, who fails to notify law enforcement that a subscriber is using the Web site, bulletin board, or forum to post or transmit child pornographic images is guilty of a Class A misdemeanor (A.C.A. 5-27-604).

A 2003 addition to the Arkansas obscenity statute, A.C.A. 5-68-502 (Unlawful Acts), requires commercial establishments to cover the lower two-thirds of displayed materials (usually book or magazine covers) deemed harmful to minors. Another part of this statute, that material harmful to minors be segregated such that minors could not have access to it, was amended in 2007 by Act 579, which deleted the segregation requirement and added language specifying that material harmful to minors is not considered to have been displayed if such material is not contained on the front cover, back cover, or binding of the displayed material.

Another technique used to regulate pornography is to establish zoning ordinances that either ban or govern the placement of sexually oriented businesses. In 2004, the City of Conway joined various other Arkansas communities with such ordinances, as it banned businesses such as adult arcades and nude model studios; the Conway ordinance also prohibits adult-oriented businesses from operating within 1,000 feet of places such as churches, schools, and public parks, and it keeps adult-oriented businesses at least 500 feet from residential areas (Hillen, 2004).

## Cases

Most of the reported obscenity cases involving Arkansas obscenity law have involved allegedly obscene films, although there have been a handful of cases involving printed matter. Additionally, questions have arisen about the promotion of obscenity, the regulation of topless entertainment establishments, and the use of children in sexual situations.

The first Arkansas case involving films was heard in federal court, and it concerned the film "The Libertine," which had been viewed by three ministers at the Minitek Theater in Fort Smith (United Artists Theatre Circuit, Inc. v. Thompson, 1970). After the ministers told a circuit court judge what they had seen, law enforcement personnel viewed the film, obtained a search warrant, and seized it without an adversary hearing. The Federal DistrictCcourt ruled that the film should be returned, but it ordered the defendant to provide a print of the film for use in the pending prosecution concerning it. The case was appealed to the U.S. Supreme Court, which in 1973 vacated the lower court's judgment and remanded the case for further consideration in light of the *Miller v. California* ruling.

The first Arkansas Supreme Court case involving films was unusual because it involved charges that depiction of nudity in a motion picture violated the nudism section of the obscenity statute (Mini-Art Operating Co., Inc. v. State, 1972). The court reversed the lower court's ruling, noting that if filmed depictions of nudity were held to violate the statute prohibiting nudism, then depictions of violence on film would have to be viewed as violations of assault statutes.

Another case heard by the court in 1972 concerned a procedural aspect of confiscating allegedly obscene films (Bullard v. State). In this case, the conviction of the manager of the Capri Theater in Texarkana, Ark., was overturned because the constable who arrested the manager also took the film, "The Affairs of Aphrodite," without a preliminary adversary hearing to independently determine the obscene quality of the film. This was similar to the federal ruling noted above.

A year later, the court decided another procedural question involving the appropriateness of the statute being applied to prohibit the showing of an allegedly obscene film (Southland Theatres, Inc. v. State, 1973). In this case, a statute prohibiting roadhouses from being public nuisances was invoked in chancery court against a North Little Rock theater, but the Arkansas Supreme Court said criminal charges should have been brought in circuit court.

Another case involving films began when movies and peep show machines were confiscated from the Paris Bookstore in Hot Springs (Gibbs v. State, 1974). Obscenity convictions in the lower court were overturned by the Arkansas Supreme Court because there had been no adversary hearings prior to the warrantless search and seizure that yielded the evidence which convicted the defendant of possessing obscene materials.

In 1974, the Arkansas Supreme Court upheld obscenity convictions of the owners of the Adult Cinema in Little Rock (Herman v. State). The convictions were challenged in part on grounds that the Arkansas obscenity law did not contain a provision that social value was a redeeming quality for allegedly obscene films, but the court held that the U.S. Supreme Court no longer accepted social value as a part of the test of obscenity.

In 1975, one defendant's conviction for selling an obscene motion picture was reversed when the Arkansas Supreme Court ruled there was insufficient evidence that one of the defendants had knowledge the film she had sold was obscene (Fortner v. State). "Guilty knowledge" (*scienter*), the court said, was required to sustain a conviction, and that, the court added, had to be more than a mere belief that the knowledge was present.

Three other film-related cases in the 1970s challenged the obscenity state on various grounds. In *Smith v. State* (1975), the Arkansas Supreme Court ruled that the statute was not overly broad. In *Buck v. Steel* (1978), the court held that certain amendments to the law had not repealed the section that made it a crime to show obscene films for free. In this case, Buck had shown an allegedly obscene film to the Glenwood High School football team. One year later, Buck won an Arkansas Supreme Court decision that mere private possession of an obscene film was not illegal (Buck v. State, 1979). This portion of the criminal statute, however, remains on the books.

In 1980, a federal court did strike down three parts of the Arkansas obscenity law (Wild Cinemas of Little Rock, Inc. v. Bentley). The court ruled that nudity was not the same as obscenity, that touching specifically listed parts of the body was not necessarily sexual conduct, and that sexual excitement was not, in itself, obscene.

In 1981, the Arkansas Supreme Court affirmed an obscenity conviction of the company that owned the Century Stereo Theater in Little Rock (Century Theaters, Inc. v. State). In this case, the company was convicted of promoting obscene material because its theater contained one-person booths where patrons could watch peep shows of hard-core sexual conduct involving homosexual and heterosexual activity.

Allegedly obscene printed materials were first challenged under anti-obscenity laws in 1943, in a case involving a conviction for exhibiting nude photographs in public (Hadley v. State). Hadley had taken some photographs of nude men, women, and children, and he had sold them to a magazine titled *Sunshine and Health.* When the magazine entered the state, Hadley was arrested. The Arkansas Supreme Court upheld his conviction.

More than two decades later, several defendants were convicted of causing a variety of men's magazines to be brought into Jefferson County (*Gent* v. State, 1965). Both the trial court and the Arkansas Supreme Court ruled that the magazines were obscene because they were not compatible with community standards. On appeal to the U.S. Supreme Court in 1967, however, the decisions were reversed because in that pre-*Miller* period, prosecutors had to show that obscene materials were utterly without redeeming social value, which was nearly impossible to demonstrate.

In 1970, a wholesale magazine distributor that operated one retail outlet (a news stand) in Fort Smith tried to convince the Arkansas Supreme Court to enjoin the mayor of Fort Smith from prosecuting its Fort Smith agent under the obscenity statute (S & S News Agency, Inc. v. Freeze). The court, however, said that asking for immunity from further prosecutions for all subsequent issues of magazines the news stand might sell was unwarranted.

Two additional cases, decided a decade apart, concerned convictions for selling obscene literature and periodicals. In the first case, *Burns v. State* (1974), the Arkansas Supreme Court upheld the convictions because it did not find the Arkansas obscenity statute vague and it did not find that the statute needed to have a *scienter* requirement to be constitutional. In the second case, *Baird v. State* (1984), the court upheld the conviction of the Texarkana, Ark., State Line Bookstore manager but reversed the convictions of the bookstore's employees. The manager had sold two obscene periodicals to police officers, but the employees also were arrested after the police confiscated 47 different magazines without first obtaining a warrant.

Two years later, in *4000 Asher, Inc. v. State* (1986), the court upheld obscenity convictions that had stemmed from an arrest involving the Asher Book Mart. The defendants did not dispute the alleged obscenity of the books, magazines, and movies they were selling, but they did argue that they were denied equal protection under the law because they were being held to a higher standard than employees of movie houses. The court ruled that bookstore clerks often can play a role in the sale of pornography, whereas movie theater employees play no part in inducing patrons to come to the theater. The court also said that exemptions for employees of schools, museums, and libraries were reasonable.

Three other cases involving promotion of obscene materials were heard by the Arkansas Supreme Court from 1987 to 1990. In Dunlap v. State (1987), the court upheld a conviction even though the defendant argued that the obscenity statute was void for vagueness. Additionally, the court found no problem with the trial court's refusal to let the defendant present to the jury evidence concerning the acceptability of pornographic materials in the Little Rock area. In 1989, the court ruled that statements made by the trial court judge required a mistrial (Oglesby v. State), and in 1990, the court affirmed another conviction of Allen Dunlap for promoting obscene material (Dunlap v. State). In this case, the court rejected Dunlap's contention that the obscenity statute was void because it did not define *scienter*.

In 1992, a Hot Springs, Ark., ordinance regulating sexually oriented businesses was found unconstitutional because it did not guarantee a speedy determination of eligibility for a license to operate such a business (Orrell v. City of Hot Springs). The Arkansas Supreme Court said the ordinance lacked adequate procedural safeguards because licensing depended upon approval by various city agencies without specifying a time limit for such approval. This, according to the court, was an impermissible prior restraint.

In another area, one case involving children and obscenity came before the Arkansas Supreme Court in 1993 (Richardson v. State). In this case, the defendant was convicted of one count of engaging children in sexually explicit conduct for use in visual or print media. On appeal, the court reversed the lower court ruling and dismissed the charge because the state had not met the requirement of proof that the act was done for profit.

After the *Richardson* decision, the General Assembly in 1995 amended the definitions section (A.C.A. 5-27-302 (3)) of this sexual exploitation statute and removed the requirement that a profit motive be shown in order to obtain a conviction.

# References

## Publications

Hillen, M. (2004, Feb. 25). Conway approves restrictions for adult-themed business. *Arkansas Democrat-Gazette*, p. 12B.

Rommel, S.F. (1994). The Arkansas obscenity doctrine: Its establishment and evolution. *Arkansas Law Review, 47*(2), 393-447.

## Cases

Ashcroft v. Free Speech Coalition, 535 U.S. 234 (2002).

Baird v. State, 12 Ark. App. 71, 671 S.W.2d 191 (1984).

Buck v. State, 265 Ark. 434, 578 S.W.2d 579 (1979).

Buck v. Steel, 263 Ark. 249, 564 S.W.2d 215 (1978).

Bullard v. State, 252 Ark. 806, 481 S.W.2d 363 (1972).

Burns v. State, 256 Ark. 1008, 512 S.W.2d 928 (1974).

Century Theaters, Inc. v. State, 274 Ark. 484, 625 S.W.2d 511 (1981).

Dunlap v. State, 292 Ark. 51, 728 S.W.2d 155, *cert. denied*, Dunlap v. Arkansas, 484 U.S. 852 (1987).

Dunlap v. State, 303 Ark. 222, 795 S.W.2d 920 (1990), *cert. denied*, 498 U.S. 1121 (1991).

Fortner v. State, 258 Ark. 591, 528 S.W.2d 378 (1975).

4000 Asher, Inc. v. State, 290 Ark. 8, 716 S.W.2d 190 (1986).

*Gent* v. State, 239 Ark. 474, 393 S.W.2d 219 (1965), *rev'd sub. nom.*, Redrup v. New York, 386 U.S. 767 (1967).

Gibbs v. State, 255 Ark. 997, 504 S.W.2d 719 (1974).

Hadley v. State, 205 Ark. 1027, 172 S.W.2d 237 (1943).

Herman v. State, 256 Ark. 840, 512 S.W.2d 93 (1974, *cert. denied*, Herman v. Arkansas, 420 U.S. 953 (1975).

Miller v. California, 413 U.S. 15 (1973).

Mini-Art Operating Co., Inc. v. State, 253 Ark. 364, 486 S.W.2d 8 (1972).

Oglesby v. State, 299 Ark. 403, 773 S.W.2d 443 (1989).

Orrell v. City of Hot Springs, 311 Ark. 301, 844 S.W.2d 310 (1992).

Richardson v. State, 314 Ark. 512, 863 S.W.2d 572 (1993).

S & S News Agency, Inc. v. Freeze, 247 Ark. 1078, 449 S.W.2d 404 (1970).

Smith v. State, 258 Ark. 549, 528 S.W.2d, 360 (1975).

Southland Theatres, Inc. v. State, 254 Ark. 192, 492 S.W.2d 421 (1973).

United Artists Theatre Circuit, Inc. v. Thompson, 316 F. Supp. 815 (W.D. Ark. 1970), *vacated*, Thompson v. United Artists Theatre Circuit, Inc., 413 U.S. 903 (1973).

Wild Cinemas of Little Rock, Inc. v. Bentley, 499 F. Supp. 655 (E.D. Ark. 1980).

## Statutes

Arkansas Protection of Children Against Exploitation Act of 1979, A.C.A. 5-27-301 *et seq.* (1987).

Computer Crimes Against Minors Act, A.C.A. 5-27-601 *et seq.* (1987).

Defenses, A.C.A. 5-68-308 (1987).

Definitions (Arkansas Law on Obscenity), A.C.A. 5-68-403 (1987).

Definitions (Selling or Loaning Pornography to Minors), A.C.A. 5-68-501 (1987).

Definitions (Sexual Exploitation of Children Generally), A.C.A. 5-27-302 (1987).

Definitions (State Standards Defining and Regulating Obscenity), A.C.A. 5-68-302 (1987).

Definitions (Use of Children in Sexual Performance), A.C.A. 5-68-401 (1987).

Employing or Consenting to Use of Child in Sexual Performance), A.C.A. 5-27-402 (1987).

Engaging Children in Sexually Explicit Conduct for Use in Visual or Print Medium, A.C.A. 5-27-303 (1987).

Failure to Report Computer Child Pornography, A.C.A. 5-27-604 (1987).

Good Faith Defense, A.C.A. 5-27-404 (1987).

Mailable Matter Subject to Provisions of Subchapter, A.C.A. 5-68-404 (1987).

Nudism, A.C.A. 5-68-204 (1987).

Obscene Films (Exhibiting, Selling, etc.), A.C.A. 5-68-203 (1987).

Obscene Performance at A Live Public Show (Committing), A.C.A. 5-68-305 (1987).

Obscenity, A.C.A. 5-68-201 *et seq.* (1987).

Pandering or Possessing Visual or Print Medium Depicting Sexually Explicit Conduct Involving A Child, A.C.A. 5-27-304 (1987).

Possession Creates A Presumption, A.C.A. 5-68-415 (1987).

Possession, Sale, or Distribution, A.C.A. 5-68-405 (1987).

Producing, Directing, or Promoting Sexual Performance, A.C.A. 5-27-403 (1987).

Promoting Obscene Materials, A.C.A. 5-68-303 (1987).

Promoting Obscene Performance, A.C.A. 5-68-304 (1987).

Public Display of Obscenity, A.C.A. 5-68-205 (1987).

Publicly Displaying Obscene Material for Advertising Purposes, A.C.A. 5-68-306 (1987).

Sale or Possession of Literature Rejected by U.S. Mails, A.C.A. 5-68-202 (1987).

Unlawful Acts, A.C.A. 5-68-502 (1987).

Chapter 9

# Commercial Speech and other Business Concerns

Various Arkansas state statutes and local ordinances govern commercial speech in Arkansas. The statutes most likely to affect the mass media are described below, as are several commercial speech and media-related business cases.

## Advertising Statutes

As might be expected, the State of Arkansas prohibits false advertising (A.C.A. 5-37-515) as well as deceptive trade practices (A.C.A. 4-88-107). The latter prohibition makes it a crime to knowingly make a false representation as to the characteristics and qualities of goods or services, but it also prohibits disparaging the goods, services, or business of another by false or misleading representation of fact.

Additionally, the deceptive trade practices section forbids bait-and-switch advertising, which it describes as an attractive but insincere offer to sell a product or service. Furthermore, this section prohibits false representations concerning the ways solicited charitable contributions will be spent, and it warns against "knowingly taking advantage of a consumer who is reasonably unable to protect his or her interest because of physical infirmity, ignorance, illiteracy, inability to understand the language of the agreement, or a similar factor."

In 2003, the Arkansas General Assembly added to the Deceptive Trade Practices code Subchapter 6, the Unsolicited Commercial and Sexually Explicit Electronic Mail Fair Practices Act (A.C.A. 4-88-601 *et seq.*). This law provides for the thorough identification of the sender of unsolicited commercial and sexually explicit electronic mail, clear identification in the subject line that the mail is adult advertising, and a convenient and free mechanism for the recipient to notify the sender not to send any other electronic mail to the recipient.

While there are several advertising statutes that identify guidelines for professionals such as accountants, attorneys, and dentists, only the one specifying attorneys forbids a form of active solicitation (A.C.A. 16-22-213). This statute states, "No attorney shall use the printed media or broadcast media, cable television, or any other medium to directly solicit clients or encourage litigation in this state. Attorneys may utilize the [print and broadcast] media and all other media for advertising their areas of practice or expertise, fees, addresses, phone numbers, and as otherwise permitted by the Arkansas Supreme Court."

In 1999, the Arkansas Supreme Court revised several of the Arkansas Model Rules of Professional Conduct, several of which refer to advertising by lawyers (*In re* Amendent of the Arkansas Model Rules of Professional Conduct). Rule 7.2, section (e), now reads as follows:

> Advertisements may include photographs, voices or images of the lawyers who are members of the firm who will actually perform the services. If advertisements utilize actors or other individuals, those persons shall be clearly and conspicuously identified by name and relationship to the advertising lawyer or law firm and shall not mislead or create an unreasonable expectation about the results the lawyer may be able to obtain. Clients or former clients shall not be used in any manner whatsoever in advertisements. Dramatization in any advertisement is prohibited.

In 2009, Act 310 of the Arkansas General Assembly amended A.C.A. 7-1-103(a)(7) (Elections – Miscellaneous Misdemeanors) to require the words "Paid Political Advertisement" or "Paid Political Ad" in "... all articles, statements, or communications appearing in any newspaper printed or circulated in this state intended or calculated to influence the vote of any elector in any election and for the publication of which a consideration is paid or to be paid." Such material appearing in any radio, television, or any other electronic medium must include the same notice, as well as including the identity of "the true sponsor of the advertisement."

# Commercial Speech Cases

The first reported commercial speech case to be heard by the Arkansas Supreme Court involved lower court convictions for peddling religious items without a license in the City of Harrison (Cook v. City of Harrison, 1929). The Supreme Court upheld the convictions because it believed localities had a right to regulate business transactions, regardless of whether the materials in question were religious in nature.

The next reported case, in which two lower court cases were combined at the Arkansas Supreme Court, concerned the constitutionality of two ordinances in Fort Smith (Cole v. City of Fort Smith, 1941). One question was whether the city could require a license of people wishing to distribute handbills or circulars. The court ruled that the ordinance was unconstitutional because it did not distinguish between the distribution of free items and items for sale, although the plaintiffs in this case, Jehovah's Witnesses, were selling religious materials.

The other question in this case was whether another ordinance could require people to obtain a license to peddle items in the city. On this point, the court ruled in favor of the city, despite the fact that the Jehovah's Witnesses in this instance were going house to house and giving away books if residents could not afford to buy them.

It was more than 50 years before another distribution question came before the Arkansas Supreme Court, but this, too, challenged the constitutionality of a Fort Smith ordinance governing handbill distribution. Although the court, in *dicta*, noted that the ordinance was constitutional, it declined a formal holding of that nature because the specific issue had not been raised at trial (Laudan v. State, 1995).

Six cases from the 1970s and 1980s, five heard by the Arkansas Supreme Court and one decided by the 8th U.S. Circuit Court of Appeals, fall into the commercial speech category. The first case heard by the Arkansas Supreme Court involved a city ordinance regulating billboards and other signs (American Television Co. Inc. v. City of Fayetteville, 1973). The facts of the case were that Fayetteville had passed a 97-page zoning ordinance requiring many changes in the size and placement of billboards the Donrey Outdoor Advertising Company and the Tri-State Reality Company operated under permits obtained from the city prior to passage of the ordinance. The billboard owners felt the changes required an inordinate financial burden, and that not complying with the ordinance would deprive them of property without due process and without adequate compensation. The Arkansas Supreme Court reversed the lower court's decision and held that the plaintiffs had a right to demand an equity decision for these changes.

As a result, the pleadings were amended to test the constitutionality of the city's restrictions on the size and locations of billboards. The trial court upheld the restrictions and the billboard owners appealed. In 1983, the Arkansas Supreme Court ruled that the city's attempts to control the size, shape, and placement of signs did not violate the First Amendment because the restrictions did not attempt to control communicative aspects of the signs (Donrey Communications v. City of Fayetteville).

Between hearing these two cases involving the same parties arguing different points of law, the Arkansas Supreme Court heard another case related to the Fayetteville sign ordinance (Board of Adjustment of Fayetteville v. Osage Oil & Transportation, Inc., 1975). In recognizing that ordinances limiting the right to maintain billboards are not unreasonable as a matter of law, the court said that outdoor advertising signs are not maintainable as a matter of right, and that such signs have been prohibited altogether.

The fourth Arkansas Supreme Court case during this period concerned attorney advertising that listed an initial consultation fee of only $10 and mentioned other available legal services without corresponding prices (Eaton v. Supreme Court of Arkansas, 1980). The court ruled that the advertisement in question failed to provide sufficient information for potential clients trying to make an informed decision. The court also noted the advertisement had been included in a packet with other advertisements, most of which were discount coupons for local businesses, and thus it was impermissible because it could have been perceived as a solicitation of discount legal services.

The 8th U.S. Circuit Court of Appeals case began when a group of merchants in Nebraska challenged their state's law prohibiting the use, sale, and manufacture of drug paraphernalia, and advertising promoting the sale of objects designed or intended for use as drug paraphernalia (Casbach, Inc. v. Thone, 1981). The merchants said the law was vague and overly broad.

The court, noting that commercial speech enjoyed less constitutional protection than noncommercial speech, upheld the statute. It also said that commercial speech which promotes an illegal activity may be restricted without subjecting the restriction to scrutiny under a balancing test. Earlier, a lower court also had ruled against the merchants (Casbach, Inc. v. Thone, 1980).

During the next decade, a commercial speech question about a state agency's regulatory powers over promotional practices of utilities reached the Court of Appeals of Arkansas (Arkansas Electric Cooperative Corporation v. Arkansas Public Service Commission, 1993). Among the issues in question was whether the Public Service Commission could require that a public utility obtain approval from the Commission before the utility engaged in promotional practices. The court held that requiring approval was not equivalent to a blanket prohibition of promotional practices.

A second issue raised by the Electric Cooperative was whether the Commission could require that a utility's proposed promotional practices benefit rate payers in the aggregate, instead of merely the customers of the single utility making the proposal. The court upheld the requirement, noting that it allowed the Commission to protect the overall public interest rather than the interest of just one segment of the public.

The last issue the court dealt with in this case concerned the burdens of inefficiency and delays that the Electric Cooperative said utilities would encounter if the regulation was upheld. On this issue, the court said that rules are not invalid simply because they may work a hardship or create inconveniences.

In 1991, the Eighth Circuit Court of Appeals heard a case involving a city's authority to limit a TV cable company's right to place advertising on its system. The City of Paragould authorized Paragould Cablevision, Inc., to establish a second competing franchise within the city. The franchise agreement limited "additional income producing activities, such as advertising." Paragould Cablevision argued that the limitation violated its First Amendment right to engage in commercial speech and its right to equal protection because no such limitation had been placed upon the first franchise. The Court of Appeals held that by entering the agreement, Paragould Cablevision had bargained away its free speech rights to advertise and could not subsequently invoke the First Amendment to recapture a surrendered right (Paragould Cablevision, Inc. v. City of Paragould).

In 2001, the Arkansas Supreme Court was asked to determine whether a rule created by the Arkansas Board of Chiropractic Examiners unconstitutionally violated the First Amendment protection of free speech (Culpepper v. Arkansas Board of Chiropractic Examiners). The rule proscribed in-person solicitation of potential clients, and Culpepper had employed a telemarketing firm to inform the public of his availability. When the Board placed Culpepper on a one-year probation for violating the rule, he sought judicial relief. Reversing the decision of the Pulaski County Circuit Court, the Arkansas Supreme Court said the regulation failed the commercial speech test devised by the U.S. Supreme court in Central Hudson Gas & Electric v. Public Service Commission (1980). Specifically, the Arkansas Supreme Court said the regulation did not detail how it furthered an articulated governmental interest, and it was not sufficiently narrowly tailored to protect governmental interests without overly burdening Culpepper's First Amendment rights.

## Media Business Cases

Two other areas of interest to the mass media are taxation and monopoly, and there are three reported modern conflicts in Arkansas involving these topics. In the first, described in Chapter 2, the U.S. Supreme Court struck down an Arkansas sales tax that applied to general interest magazines, while exempting publications such as newspapers and special interest journals (Arkansas Writers' Project v. Ragland, 1987). The Court found that discriminatory taxes based on content, even when there is no intent to censor, violate the First Amendment.

A second media taxation case was decided by the Arkansas Supreme Court in 1990 (Medlock v. Pledger). Pledger, the Arkansas Commissioner of Revenues, had been sued because a 1987 Arkansas law had levied a sales tax on cable television service without extending the tax to other forms of mass communication. By the time the court heard the case, the Arkansas General Assembly had amended the law to include other mass media, so the court ruled that the law now was constitutional, but that revenue collected prior to the 1989 amendment had been collected illegally.

In the only reported modern media monopoly case litigated in Arkansas, a Federal District Court judge decided that Connecticut-based Thomson Newspapers could not sell the *Northwest Arkansas Times* to a company named NAT L.C., because NAT L.C. was controlled by another company that controlled *The Morning News of Northwest Arkansas*, which was in a circulation and advertising battle with a third paper in the locale, the *Benton County Daily Record* (Community Publishers, Inc. v. Donrey Corp., 1995). Community Publishers, Inc. of Bentonville, owner of the *Benton County Daily Record*, challenged the sale as a violation of federal antitrust laws.

The district court judge in this case issued two opinions that, based on market conditions, the sale was illegal and ownership of the *Northwest Arkansas Times* should revert to the previous owner. In 1998, a three-judge panel of the 8th U.S. Circuit Court of Appeals upheld the district court's order, noting that the original sale created a reasonable probability that competition in the local Northwest Arkansas newspaper business would be substantially lessened.

Finally, in an unreported case that received state-wide publicity (Arkansas Gazette Co. v. Little Rock Newspapers, Inc.), a Federal District Court jury, on March 26, 1986, decided that Little Rock Newspapers, Inc., owner of the *Arkansas Democrat*, had not violated statutes prohibiting unfair competition when it offered free classified advertising to readers during a circulation war with the *Arkansas Gazette* (Wells, 1986). The newspaper war continued until October 1991, when the Gannett Corporation, which then owned the *Gazette*, closed the newspaper and sold its assets to owners of the *Arkansas Democrat*.

# References

## Publications

Wells, G. (1986, March 27). Antitrust verdict favors *Democrat. Arkansas Gazette*, p. A1.

## Cases

American Television Co. Inc. v. City of Fayetteville, 253 Ark. 760, 489 S.W.2d 754 (1973).

Arkansas Electric Cooperative Corporation v. Arkansas Public Service Commission, 42 Ark. App. 198, 856 S.W.2d 880 (1993).

Arkansas Gazette Co. v. Little Rock Newspapers, Inc. (unreported) (U.S. District Court for the Eastern District of Arkansas, March 26, 1986).

Arkansas Writers' Project v. Ragland, 481 U.S. 221 (1987).

Board of Adjustment of Fayetteville v. Osage Oil & Transportation, Inc., 258 Ark. 91, 522 S.W.2d 836 (1975).

Casbach, Inc. v. Thone, 512 F. Supp. 474 (D. Neb. 1980), *affirmed*, 651 F.2d 551 (8th Cir. 1981).

Central Hudson Gas & Electric v. Public Service Commission, 447 U.S. 557 (1980).

Cole v. City of Fort Smith, 202 Ark. 614, 151 S.W.2d 1000 (1941).

Community Publishers, Inc. v. Donrey Corp., 882 F. Supp. 138 (W.D. Ark. 1995), *clarified*, 892 F. Supp. 1146 (W.D. Ark. 1995), *affirmed sub nom.*, Community Newspapers, Inc. v. DR Partners, 139 F.3d 1180 (1998).

Cook v. City of Harrison, 180 Ark. 546, 21 S.W.2d 966 (1929).

Culpepper v. Arkansas Board of Chiropractic Examiners, 343 Ark. 467, 36 S.W.3d 335 (2001).

Deitsch v. Tillery, 309 Ark. 401, 833 S.W.2d 760 (1992).

Donrey Communications v. City of Fayetteville, 280 Ark. 408, 660 S.W.2d 900 (1983), *cert. denied*, 466 U.S. 959 (1984).

Eaton v. Supreme Court of Arkansas, 270 Ark. 573, 607 S.W.2d 55 (1980), *cert. denied*, 450 U.S. 966 (1981).

Hudspeth v. State, 349 Ark. 315, 78 S.W.3d 99 (2002).

Jegley v. Picado, 349 Ark. 600, 80 S.W.3d 332 (2002).

Laudan v. State, 322 Ark. 58, 907 S.W.2d 131 (1995).

Medlock v. Pledger, 301 Ark. 483, 785 S.W.2d 202 (1990).

Northport Health Services, Inc. v. Owens, 82 Ark. App. 355, 107 S.W.3d 889 (2003).

Paragould Cablevision Inc. v. City of Paragould, 930 F.2d 1310 (1991).

Walley v. State, 353 Ark, 586, 112 S.W.3d 349 (2003).

Wal-Mart Stores, Inc. v. Lee, 348 Ark. 707, 74 S.W.3d 634 (2002).

## Statutes and Court Rules

Advertising (Attorneys), A.C.A. 16-22-213 (1987).

Deceptive and Unconscionable Trade Practices Generally, A.C.A. 4-88-107 (1987).

Elections – Miscellaneous Misdemeanors (Paid Political Advertising), A.C.A. 7-1-103(a)(7) (1987).

False Advertising Generally, A.C.A. 5-37-515 (1987).

*In re* Amendment of the Arkansas Model Rules of Professional Conduct, Rules 7.1, 7.2, and 7.3 — Information About Legal Services, 337 Ark. 643 (1999).

Unsolicited Commercial and Sexually Explicit Electronic Mail Fair Practices Act, A.C.A. 4-88-601 *et seq.* (1987).

# Cases Index

## Y



## Z

# Subject Index

## A



## B

## C



## D

## P



## Q



## R



## S

# T



# U



# V



# W

www.ingramcontent.com/pod-product-compliance
Lightning Source LLC
Chambersburg PA
CBHW052109230326
41599CB00054B/4996